COURTHOUSE DESIGN

THE FIRST INTERNATIONAL CONFERENCE

Cosponsors

The American Institute of Architects,
Committee on Architecture for Justice

U.S. Federal Courts

National Center for State Courts

Writers

Simpson Lawson

Fred Jordan

Robin Tunnicliff

Publisher

The American Institute of Architects

Washington, D.C.

AIA Press
The American Institute of Architects
1735 New York Avenue, NW
Washington, DC 20006-5292

Library of Congress Cataloging-in-Publication Data
Lawson, Simpson F.
    Courthouse design : the first international conference / Simpson
Lawson, Fred Jordan, Robin Tunnicliff.
        P.   cm.
    "The U.S. Federal Courts, The American Institute of Architects
Committee on Architecture for Justice, the National Center for State
Courts."
    ISBN 1-55835-118-3 (paper) : $20.00
    1. Courthouses--Congresses. 2. Architecture, Modern--20th
century--Congresses. I. Jordan, Fred. II Tunnicliff, Robin.
III. American Institute of Architects. Committee on Architecture
for Justice. IV. National Center for State Courts.
V. International Conference on Courthouse Design (1st : 1992 :
Washington, D.C.) VI. Title.
NA4470.L38   1993
725' . 15--dc20   93-28652
                                                                    CIP

Publication Design
Renée Boudreau Design, Sterling, Va.

Cover Photo
Old Courthouse, Williamsburg, Va.
© Colonial Williamsburg
Reproduced with the permission of
The Colonial Williamsburg Foundation

INTRODUCTION

The First International Conference on Courthouse Design came out of the development of the U.S. Courts Design Guide (USCDG) issued by the U.S. federal courts in 1991. In researching information for the guide, Federal Judges Michael Kanne and Douglas Woodlock and Gerald Thacker, of the Space and Facilities Department of the Administrative Office of the U.S. Courts, noted that counterparts in state courts and in other countries were struggling with many of the issues addressed in the USCDG: the effect on courthouse design of growing caseload, of technolgy, of security concerns, and of project management and financing. The three approached Michael Cohn and Elisabeth Moller, staff of The American Institute of Architects Committee on Architecture for Justice (AIA/CAJ), about working together to create a forum in which architects, planners, designers, judges, and administrators could come together to discuss problems and solutions in these areas. After the initial contact, the groups agreed to cosponsor the effort and, after further discussion, invited the National Center for State Courts (NCSC) to join them.

Representatives of the three cosponsors worked over the next two years to develop a program that would address courthouse and courtroom design issues in three areas: design, technology, and management. Within each conference track the planners identified experts to comment on hot issues such as implications of the Americans with Disabilities Act (ADA), security, long-term planning, and architect selection.

Members of the planning committee eventually included Judges Kanne and Woodlock; Thacker; Larry Sipes, Don Hardenberg, Cheng-Ming Yeh, and Wallis Daniels from the NCSC; and Michael Frawley, AIA, Ron Budzinski, AIA, Todd Phillips, AIA, Suzanne Hofer, and Melanie Miller from the AIA. The spirit of goodwill and cooperations that was evidenced at planning meetings continues today.

The same cosponsors are now working on the Second International Conference on Courthouse Design, scheduled for the fall of 1995 in San Francisco. The overwhelming success and usefulness of the first event acknowledges the need to broaden international participation in future events, to continue to identify new issues, and to revisit critical issues in light of changing technology and regulations. We hope you will join us in 1995 as we continue to explore how courts facility design evolves with the changing needs of society.

CONTENTS

COURTHOUSE DESIGN

THE FIRST INTERNATIONAL CONFERENCE

OVERVIEW

The First International Conference on Courthouse Design brought together 500 architects, judges, and court administrators from across the United States and six other countries. They met to discuss ways to replenish the aging stock of court facilities in the face of an escalating and diversifying range of judicial functions. The conference was sponsored by the United States Federal Courts, The American Institute of Architects, and the National Center for State Courts.

These prime movers in the process of building and renovating courthouses and their many ancillary structural elements convened the meeting amid growing recognition of the need to expand and improve facilities of courts of all levels. U.S. Supreme Court Chief Justice William H. Rehnquist welcomed the participants to the meeting with a reminder that "both federal and state court systems are faced with what has been described as a litigation explosion" that has strained all court systems and "the existing physical facilities in which the courts are housed."

This, he said, is forcing the federal judiciary "to embark on the largest federal construction program in our nation's history."

The chief justice summarized the short-range projections:

Each federal district is now required to develop long-range facility plans based upon future case-load projections at 5-, 10-, and 30-year intervals. The plans today predict that over 50 major new federal courthouse projects will be required by 1997, with an additional 10 major courthouse projects necessary by 2002, just 10 years from now.

In the short run, Chief Justice Rehnquist said, both federal and state courts must provide for expanding space needs in the face of severe budget constraints. In the long run, however, he added, planning must focus not simply on facilities expansion but also on innovative alternative methods of dispensing justice. Increased use of alternative dispute resolution services may change the future design needs and lead us to build justice centers instead of the familiar courthouses of the present.

Continued advances in computers and communications may lead to what people call the virtual courthouse where justice can be dispensed without all parties gathering in the same place. A renewed commitment to cooperation between the federal and state judicial systems may lead to more and more shared facilities—joint state-federal justice centers—instead of a separate one for each. Depending in part on the ideas exchanged in this and similar forums the structures in which the justice of the future is dispensed may look very different from the court-houses we see today.

The conference did indeed offer a vision of justice centers of the future, but not a consensus vision.

"In a society that is increasingly heterogeneous," said Kenneth Starr, solicitor general of the United States, these justice centers "should be places that are warmly hospitable to the citizenry, not just lawyers, jurors, and press persons." Starr, a former federal appellate judge, suggested that justice centers should contain places where alternative forms of dispute resolution can take place. "What we need," he argued, "is design that provides facilities for early evaluation of disputes," a process that would determine issues that might be settled by some form of arbitration. This, he maintained, would reduce "the burgeoning case load by letting judges focus their attention only on those cases that need to go to trial."

Furthermore, Starr contended, courthouses can be designed to be centers for the education of citizens about legal and judicial procedures. "We might want to think about how we could engage jurors in civic education," he said. For example, he suggested, the courthouse could contain a space where jurors could view videos about outstanding court decisions.

Judge Michael S. Kanne, of the United States Court of Appeals for the Seventh Circuit, concurred with Starr's advocacy of a design that would create space for alternate forms of dispute resolution. But, he said, his vision of the courthouse of the future was not as "warm and fuzzy" as the one pictured by Starr. "The system is purposefully adversarial," said Kanne, who served as both a state and federal trial judge before joining the appellate bench. Trials, he asserted, are "controlled conflict. They are not meant to be warm, relaxed, and informal."

The complexity of the challenge for designers should not be underestimated, said Professor Charles T. Goodsell, of the Center for Public Administration and Policy at Virginia Polytechnic Institute and State University. "We need to realize how hard it is to have something as exalted and vague as a vision translated into something as concrete and everyday as a building," he said.

A Temple With a "Populist Presence"

Goodsell urged that courthouse design express conflicting, or non-parallel, values. Designers, he said, should provide both legal and populist symbols. "The courthouse needs to be a temple of the law, an elitist notion in the finest sense. In this sense the judge is the superior authority. We also need a populist presence," expressed in a different set of symbols and in such pragmatic measures as adequate public seating for trials that attract widespread interest.

Bill Lacy, FAIA, the conference keynote speaker, viewed the challenge of courthouse building from the perspective of a consultant who is internationally known for convening and guiding architectural selection panels for courthouse construction. In discussing the responsibilities of courthouse designers, he reflected on his experience in enhancing the design and function of federal buildings as the first director of arts and architecture for the National Endowment for the Arts. He also drew on his memory of courthouses as stable centers of civic and commercial activity in cities and county seats throughout the nation, including his hometown of Medill, Okla.

Lacy, an architect himself, declared that "courthouses offer an extraordinary opportunity for architects because they provide possibilities architects love to deal with: spaces that are both ennobling and soothing. Courthouses—like churches, synagogues, and hospitals—test the full measure of architects' talents to deal with people in states of extreme vulnerability. They require the making of spaces that are symbolic, that stretch back through time and attempt—with a sense of stability and durability—to reassure troubled minds and to raise the ideal of a world that aspires to a higher order of meaning and beauty."

Lacy, who chaired a committee that selected the architect for the new Israeli Supreme Court, concluded on a reassuring note:

"I think we are poised to build a new generation of courthouses based on new ideas and new technology, and I hope we can accept the fact that models from the past will only be guidelines to serve us. We need to find new ways to express the central importance of law and order and an architectural expression that will aspire not to minimum standards but to the highest levels of our ability to build well and beautifully, just as they did in ancient Greece and just as they did in the county courthouse in Medill, Oklahoma."

Chief Justice Rehnquist's reminder about the impact of computers and communications on judicial procedure was frequently reiterated. Conferees were reminded in virtually every session of the need to adapt courthouses for a broad range of existing and anticipated electronic hardware and software. Nevertheless, a legion of panelists counterbalanced the concern to stay ahead of the curve of progress

Supreme Court Chief Justice William H. Rehnquist

Photographer: Lynne Lewicki
© The American Institute of Architects

in communications with pleas to respect—even inspire awe for—traditions, symbols, and forms historically associated with the majesty of the courts. "The courthouse to most Americans still calls up an image of an accessible, friendly, often odd-looking building on a town square with a steeple or clock tower," said architectural historian William Seale in an oral essay on the historical context for the federal courthouse. Seale was careful to note that federal courthouses, seldom central features of urban centers, haven't ever fit this stereotype. "Yet," he added, "we cannot entirely dispel the image, in a culture as old as we have become. Its power may well hold some meaning for the present."

The Effect of Legislation and Social Change

The conference agenda was broad. In assessing strategies for replacing, renovating, and augmenting inadequate quarters of the courts, the conferees weighed the impact of the Americans with Disabilities Act, the aging population and other demographic trends, and recent immigration laws and the changing ethnic patterns they have fostered.

They discussed the advantages of expansion of functions in the court-house (day-care centers, educational facilities, etc.) and they examined in minute detail architect Arthur Erickson's urbane Vancouver court complex. This mega courthouse, which houses multiple functions, preserves its beaux-arts predecessor, and brings a greening to Vancouver's downtown grid that, remarkably, gives the massive complex what historian Seale called a "village-like ring."

The participants pondered the impact of changes imposed on new construction and major renovation, not just from increased case loads, but from changes in patterns of dispute resolution, and technological advances.

Not surprisingly, management tools have increased in complexity in direct proportion to the increasing diversity of court functions. The traditional sequence involving consensual selection of an architect, estimation of construction costs, and award of the construction contract to the lowest bidder has undergone extensive improvisation. Design competitions, once favored by communities for monumental structures such as courthouses, are often replaced by a range of developer-architect-judiciary combinations under the direction of a professional construction manager. The conference carefully explored these changing patterns.

Projections by the Federal Judiciary

Not the least of the participants' concerns was the cost of accomplishing their objectives and the prospects for meeting them. On the basis of projections made by 65 of the country's 94 federal court districts, administrators of the federal judiciary estimate that major construction or renovation will be needed in 120 locations.

Administrators of the federal courts estimate that Congress is appropriating funds for court facilities at the rate of $750 million a year. The expectation that outlays for federal courts will total $10 billion over the next 5 to 10 years was widely held by conference participants. The election of Bill Clinton a month after the conference seemed likely to raise this expectation since the president-elect advocated investments in public infrastructure during his campaign. However, John Callahan, deputy staff director of the Senate Budget Committee, reminded conference participants that the courts would be among many claimants should the next Congress approve an economic-stimulus package.

This summary touches lightly on the myriad issues raised and the solutions proposed. These issues were discussed in exhaustive detail as the conference proceeded along three separate tracks: Design, Technology, and Management.

DESIGN

In seeking insight on designing the courthouses of the future, the conference focused strongly on the past—on the judicial roots and traditions of the Colonial period and the earliest days of the new republic. Architects and jurists were almost unanimous in praising courthouses of this era as the epitome of public structures. These buildings were designed for a government that itself was designed for the people, and they reflected that ideal.

Indeed, as conference attendees learned, the newest American courthouses under design affirmatively claim descent from the paradigmatic courthouses of the colonial period. Thus, Carl Lounsbury, architectural historian for the Colonial Williamsburg Foundation, in his presentation of 18th century Virginia courthouses, focused on the one-courtroom, circa 1735 Hanover County, Va., Courthouse as an exemplar. Ironically, Lounsbury's presentation was preceded by a discussion of work in progress in the design of the new 29-courtroom, Boston Federal Courthouse, during which Harry Cobb, FAIA, founding partner of the New York architectural firm of Pei Cobb Freed & Partners, confided that he keeps a photograph of the Hanover County Courthouse before him at all times in the hopes that his contemporary work in Boston will parallel the colonial Virginia building in its public quality and in its modesty, probity, clarity, integrity, dignity, and economy of means.

Hanover County Courthouse, Hanover, Va.

Boston Federal Courthouse, Boston, Mass.

Maryland State House, Annapolis, Md.

that models from the past are only guidelines."

"In a sense there is a clean slate as to what the new American court will be like," said architectural historian William Seale in an oral essay on the federal courthouse. "Present feelings seem to point to the fact that it will not be in the dull vernacular of the faceless blocks of recent years . . ."

Arrangements: Symbolic and Functional

Few conference participants have resisted the "faceless blocks of recent years" with greater persistence than architect Allan Greenberg. Greenberg, who has offices in Washington, D.C., and Connecticut, is the designer of the State Department's diplomatic rooms and a consultant to Connecticut's chief court administrator. Designers of many newer buildings that house the courts have forgotten the public, "the raison d'etre of courthouses," Greenberg contended. "I wonder whether it isn't time to focus on the missing ingredient. Let us realize our courthouse using the architectural tradition that grew out of the American Revolution."

To illustrate his point, Greenberg cited the Maryland State House in Annapolis, the first statehouse built after the Revolution. Using standard residential elements of the time, the architects used brick and outfitted the building with porch, pediment, and windows. However, what made this house different was its symbolic dome—a powerful element used throughout history to designate public buildings. The dome atop the national Capitol, hailed by Lincoln upon its completion in 1863 as a sign the Union would stay intact, was replicated in successive years on numerous state capitols.

There were pointed reminders throughout the conference that capturing these ideals in today's courthouses does not require designers to endlessly duplicate the structural forms of the Hanover County Courthouse and some of its revered contemporaries. "I think we are poised to build a new generation of courthouses built on new technology," said architect Bill Lacy, a consultant who frequently advises architect-selection panels for courthouse projects. "I hope we accept the fact

In a session titled "Where Do I Sit?," Greenberg said the positions assigned to participants in traditional American courtrooms reflect fundamental principles of this nation's system of jurisprudence, which is unique in the world. He noted, for example, that placing the judge's bench in a center position signifies lack of bias for the prosecution on one side or the defense on the other side. Witnesses in this traditional arrangement face the contending sides, while the jury, indicative of its impartial role, is seated "off to the side."

Greenberg, author of a handbook on courthouse design for the American Bar Association, cited a report contrasting this relationship of typical courtroom elements in the United States with those of courts in Europe. The report described a court in Poland during the communist regime in which a red-robed prosecutor, the only participant robed, sits on the podium next to the judge while the defendant sits alone in the center of the courtroom. In Switzerland the jury sits behind the judge, who is also a member of the panel. In England, the accused does not sit with counsel conducting his defense but is placed in an elevated dock with a security officer.

"Particularities of American law and the massive paraphernalia by which our legal system protects the rights of the accused is beautifully mirrored in the layout of our courtrooms," Greenberg maintained. "Let us treasure this wonderful heritage. Let us recognize that by subtle manipulation we can take our traditional courtroom layout and make it function for any kind of trial and any size courtroom."

C. William Westfall, an architectural history professor at the University of Virginia, also urged architects to remember the civic elements of courthouse design. Too many post World War II structures have sacrificed public interest for artistic motivation, Westfall added.

"I am going to embrace the proposition that ways of thought in American justice and architecture that served at the founding of the country are still as useful," he said. "There is nothing more important than fulfilling the duties of citizenship. Therefore, it follows that there must be nothing more important to a nation, a state, a county, a city . . . than the facilities that allow that work to be done."

Westfall then delivered a stinging indictment of Modern architecture.

"The architect designing the courthouse no longer sets about first of all to provide a place where justice could be rendered. The modernist ways of thought have brought us architecture we find baffling at best and offensive at worst, and this cannot serve justice in America."

The Round Courtroom Is Rejected

Perhaps the most offensive Modern idea to those working in the courts is the round courtroom, an idea that evolved in the 1960s and 1970s. Typically in such courtrooms, the participants are arranged in a circle, creating an arena in the center. Advocates of this plan are seeking to signify a more egalitarian approach to judicial proceedings, said Judge Kanne. He said he hoped this notion would not become a wave of the future. "The idea that courtrooms can be designed to be user-friendly and comfortable does not comport with reality. The courtroom is not a playground. We have more practical considerations. [The final

design] really depends on the attitude of the judges [in a specific area]."

Attorney Margaret Marshall, past president of the Boston Bar Association and general counsel for Harvard University, offered a more direct condemnation of alternative designs for courtrooms.

"Please don't bring all of your new ideas into the courtroom," she admonished. "No judges sitting in the corners. I like to have the judge in front of me. I have to watch the judge all the time." While expressing a preference for traditional courtrooms, Marshall stressed that courtrooms should be able to accommodate contemporary needs, with adequate electrical outlets, provisions for using visual aids, and an abundance of telephones. (She made this plea to courthouse designers: "However many telephones you think we need, double it, then double it again.")

Above all, she said, courtrooms should have good acoustic qualities. "This is important for me, because I teach and persuade in a courtroom, and I do this mostly through oral advocacy. If those I'm trying to persuade [notably judges] can't hear me, I can't do what I'm supposed to do in a courtroom."

Form, Meaning, and the Future

The discussion's intense focus on traditional design could perhaps be attributed in part to an examination of historic motifs by New Yorker writer Brendan Gill in an after-dinner address. Gill reflected on the potential of civic design to inspire "feelings of awe, or reverence, or reassurance, even of consolation."

How, he asked, can architects express such feelings in the courthouses of the future? "Which of the architectural symbols that have been so puissant in our culture in the past can be said to remain effectual today in communities that are in desperate need of them, if indeed any symbols are likely to survive into the 21st century?"

Gill recalled a blunt warning by Senator Daniel Patrick Moynihan that "20th century America has seen the steady, persistent decline of the individual and emotional power of its buildings. This has been accompanied by the not less persistent decline of the authority of the political order."

This moved Gill to ask: "How can we restore visual and emotional power to our public buildings as we pitch headlong into the 21st century?"

Not, he suggested, with the continued revival of classicism.

"What does the ordinary citizen know today of Greek or Roman culture or the culture of the founding fathers, or the culture that lies embalmed in the darkness somewhere beyond Madonna or Magic Johnson or the mindless beast of the boombox? What is to be the design of the buildings that we have been given the opportunity to provide for our children and grandchildren? Luckily for me, my task this evening has been to ask the question, but not to furnish the answer. That task is yours to perform, and I do not envy you."

Perhaps part of the answer lies in an observation by Massachusetts architect Andrea Leers, founding principal in the Boston firm Leers, Weinzapfel Associates, whose projects include the design of new and renovated courthouses. She acknowledged the power of the courthouses of the past to symbolize both community and authority, but cautioned against rebuilding the past.

"Today, we are seeking to embody a very much more complex phenom-

The Japan Supreme Court, Tokyo, Japan

enon," she said. "We must design a courthouse that serves a more diverse and often contentious community with fewer shared beliefs and symbols. Our courthouses have multiple courtrooms embedded in large amounts of administrative space, and there is a need for a much higher level of security."

This search requires that we "broaden our perspective and look at modern courthouse exemplars around the world," she suggested, "to learn how other cultures make a connection with their own history and locale, and how they symbolize community and the meaning of law in democratic society."

Leers cited examples from India, Sweden, Japan, and Israel. The High Court of Chandigarh, designed by Le Corbusier, has a great sheltering porch both to shade the public from the severe heat of the local climate and to give a monumental order to the building and sense of progression from plaza to courtrooms. The courthouses

of Gunnar Asplund weave together elements of folk and craft traditions with modern open and flowing space. In Japan, the supreme court building designed by Shinichi Okada is interwoven with the landscape, overlooking the Imperial Palace. The new supreme court building in Jerusalem, designed by Ada and Ram Karmi, is an oasis in the desert, embedded in the stone landscape with basilica-like courtrooms and green gardens set deep within sheltering walls.

"What we are searching for in all these examples," says Leers, "is how to symbolize the court in its time and place and give it shape."

Preservation and Adaptive Use

Preserving the past—restoring sound historic structures and adapting them for contemporary use—should not be confused with Leers' admonition against rebuilding the past. But those who undertake renovation of historic courthouses have found it to be a daunting task; a job made tougher by a host of regulations. "The goal really is to rehabilitate without damaging the existing structure," said John J. Cullinane, principal in John Cullinane Associates of Washington, D.C. "Historic buildings weren't designed for today's needs. Expanding courts may really be the most viable solution."

Location is important, especially when considering whether to move a courthouse to house an expansion. "It's important to understand that retaining courts in downtowns is a demonstration of the federal or state government's commitment to urban renewal," Cullinane said. "Removal is a big statement; the community sees that as abandonment."

David Kemnitzer, of Einhorn Yaffee Prescott in Washington, D.C., said that abandoning an old building is tempting in the face of a major technological overhaul. "The courthouse's function is unchanged," he said. "New technologies have evolved—air conditioning, new computers, and even television. The population growth also strains courthouses."

Yet there are buildings so venerable that abandonment would be unthinkable. One such structure houses London's Royal Courts of Justice, England's counterpart to the great metropolitan civil courts of the United States. Scottish architect Colin Thom told fellow conferees that renovating this neo-Gothic complex to make it capable of handling increasing caseloads was the most demanding task he's ever undertaken. His detailed description of this exacting process provided a classic case study in preservation and adaptive reuse.

Through innovative planning and design, Thom was able to add 29 new courtrooms to a structure integral to London's legal heart without offending Victorian sensibilities. The cost of the whole project was about $27 million.

Thom managed to turn a parking lot about the size of two tennis courts into an 11-story building by attaching the new structure to an adjacent government building. The resulting 12 new courtrooms were built onto the older building's north and west facades, with layers of judges' chambers and clerks' offices in between. This enabled Thom to "steal a corner of each floor of the existing building to provide the new public circulation space and to use the stairs of the existing building as the fire escape from the new building."

Thom crowned the top of the new creation with weathercocks that he described as a concession to the art nouveau architectural ideals of fellow Scot Charles "Rennie" MacIntosh. "This was the only chance I was going to get as a Scot to contribute to the skyline of London, and I was blowed if I was going to waste it," he said.

Thom and colleagues from PSAA Projects of Edinburgh pinpointed two other sites for conversion—the building's crypt and east wing. The latter is still under construction.

Turning the crypt, or basement, into new courtrooms required a lot of late hours; the courts forbid any construction while they are in session. Much of the work involved stripping paint off brick walls and columns, as the main corridor had been used as a restaurant. Thom said he wanted to restore the room, painted a bright blue, to the way architect George Edmund Street envisioned it—majestic in brick.

The remaining 14 courtrooms are in the converted east wing, a four-story building attributed to Norman Shaw. Here Thom decided to gut the inside to create two separate circulation areas between the courtrooms. This meant removing the roof literally and making sure the outer walls remained intact while the interior construction was done. This project is scheduled for completion in 1993.

Looking at the slides of the Royal Courts, Thom said his heart beat a little faster. "It's relatively easy to sketch out on paper a conversion proposal that involves dramatic structural changes. But it's something else when you see on site the manifestation of your ideas."

American architects responsible for integrating spaces for today's court functions with older buildings will find valuable assistance in a comprehensive analysis the General Services Administration is compiling on properties for which it is responsible. Dale M. Lanzone, GSA's director of arts and historic preservation, said this inventory, Historic Building Preservation Plans, provides detailed profiles of buildings of architectural and historic significance and describes their condition. The information will be available for the cost of duplicating the data base that contains it.

Design Guidelines

The GSA report is part of a growing body of literature on the design of new court facilities and renovation of existing ones. The basic document for the design of federal court facilities is U.S. Courts Design Guide. Judge James Rosenbaum of the United States District Court for the District of Minnesota called this comprehensive book, issued by the United States

Alternative Comparison of Courtroom Configurations

Courtroom Planning Objectives	Center Bench Layout	Corner Bench Layout	In The Round Layout
Support the physical image of the judge as the pivotal element of the court proceeding	HIGH	MODERATE	LOW
Support the judge's control and management of all activities within the courtroom	HIGH	HIGH	LOW
Provide flexibility to accommodate a variety of types of court proceedings	MODERATE	MODERATE	LOW
Avoid excessive use of space to accommodate courtroom functions	MODERATE	MODERATE	LOW
Provide for required disabled access without undue physical complexity	MODERATE	HIGH	LOW
Provide for secure movement of in-custody defendants within the courtroom	HIGH	MODERATE	MODERATE
Provide proper line of sight between the judge and the witness	MODERATE	HIGH	HIGH
Provide proper line of sight between the jury and the witness	MODERATE	HIGH	HIGH
Provide proper line of sight between counsel and the judge, jury, and witness	MODERATE	MODERATE	HIGH
Provide for adequate spectator viewing without disruption of court proceedings	HIGH	MODERATE	LOW
Provide for proper viewing of displays and A.V. presentations by all court participants	MODERATE	HIGH	MODERATE
Provide for efficient document flow between the judge and clerk	LOW	HIGH	HIGH
Provide for efficient document flow between the counsel and clerk	HIGH	MODERATE	HIGH
Provide necessary physical separation between selective court participants	HIGH	HIGH	LOW
Provide necessary voice privacy between selective court participants	HIGH	MODERATE	LOW

Credit: Omni-Group Inc.

Judicial Conference and GSA, a "usable, workable beginning pattern" for jurisdictions planning construction and renovation. In developing the guidelines, the Judicial Conference of the United States sent federal judges to courts throughout the country and sought comments from the entire federal bench.

Federal courts differ from state, county, and municipal courts, Rosenbaum said, because most people seldom have occasion to use them. Such courts, he cautioned, should be designed for those doing business there. More importantly, the building should reflect the distinction the judiciary sees between itself and the federal government.

"The judiciary represents the Constitution. You stand independent of the government—stand in a position to judge the government." Rosenbaum said. "This defines a relationship which ought to be manifest in the court's design. The goal is a capacious, dignified structure that does have a sense of grandeur. There ought to be a message that something important is going on here."

The guidelines address a range of concerns, including the location of the bench, jury box, and witness stand; wiring, security, audibility; and requirements for judges' chambers and ancillary facilities. Variances from the standards can be granted by circuit judicial councils, Rosenbaum said.

The National Center for State Courts has also published guidelines, said Don Hardenbergh, staff associate of the Williamsburg, Va., center. *The Courthouse: A Planning and Design Guide for Court Facilities* is based on suggestions compiled over the past three years to be used as a common ground for the four groups most concerned with building a courthouse: judges, court administrators, local funding authorities, and architects. The guide is one of three documents to be published in a project funded by the State Justice Institute. The American Institute of Architects, American Bar Association, National Center for Juvenile Justice, and Conference of State Court Administrators collaborated in the project.

"Think of it as a road map," Hardenbergh said of the guide and the courthouse facilities checklist in its appendix. "It presents the problems that are going to come up, but not the solutions. You need to define it and determine your own solutions in each case."

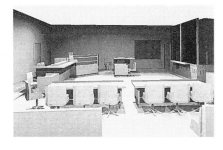

Three alternative courtroom designs

Graphics: S. Paul Warren
© Nacht & Lewis Architects,
Sacramento, Calif.

The National Center for Juvenile Justice's guidelines were a result of interviews with staffers in juvenile and family courts built during the last 10 years. The results were what director Hunter Hurst said was a "scorecard for architects."

Thirty percent of those interviewed were satisfied with their building's image, while 5 percent were totally dissatisfied; 24 percent were satisfied with accessibility (parking, signs, and courtroom size), 35 percent with security and 75 percent with life-saving escape plans. Hurst said the overwhelming majority found juvenile courtrooms too small.

Such a scorecard can help the judicial community and justice-facility architects correct user-perceived flaws or compensate for inadequacies or short-sighted judgment when they rebuild or renovate. But historical patterns suggest this might be more than a generation in the future. Increasingly, architects are involving judges and administrators in a more interactive programming process, using computer-assisted design techniques to depict graphically how court facilities will function before they undertake working drawings or build three-dimensional models. CAD methods enable programmers to respond instantly to comments by committees reviewing initial concepts and to display alternative arrangements, often gaining consensus during the same review session.

Members of a team of architects and court programming consultants involved in the planning of a new justice complex in Sacramento County, Calif., demonstrated use of these methods for an evaluation of the most prevalent concepts for courtroom layout. The presentation was made by Randall Rice, a partner in Omni-Group, Inc., Los Angeles planning consultants, and Paul Warren of the Sacramento architecture firm Nacht & Lewis. The two firms are collaborating on design of the courthouse.

During the programmatic phase of the building project, the following three generic courtroom configurations were studied to assess their advantages and disadvantages relative to court operations and administration of justice:

Center Bench: This plan entails a traditional location of the judge at a central location, with the witness stand between the judge and the jury box.

Corner Bench: This layout positions the judge's bench diagonally in the corner of the courtroom across from the jury box and adjacent to the witness stand.

"In-the-Round" Configuration: This circular arrangement puts all participants within the well of the courtroom.

Each of the three layouts was rated on how well it might perform in meeting more than a dozen functional objectives. The degree to which each of the three layouts was felt to meet the planning objectives is denoted in a range from "low" to "high" in the table, prepared by Omni-Group Inc., that appears as Table 1.

Rice demonstrated to conference attendees how the architects and their consultants used the CAD techniques not only to help their clients solve problems of physical arrangement of courtroom elements and sight lines but to plot such functions as document flow.

The CAD process, Rice said, permits the designers and court planners to develop a computer-simulated prototype that one can see rather than read about. Omni's CAD system is calibrated to insure that all input provided to the computer conforms to realistic and human dimensions. Hence, elements in a courtroom, for example, would appear as if viewed at normal eye level. The system, one of the more expensive ones available, cost $30,000. Warren, of the Nacht & Lewis staff, said software packages range from $6,000 to $8,000. The programs run on a personal computer.

Perhaps the most useful feature of CAD systems is their ability to let architects and court personnel visualize a range of scenarios in a truly interactive manner. A judge can see how the courtroom would appear from different bench heights. A clerk can trace the flow of documents throughout the courtroom. A deputy can track various paths from the holding cell to the witness stand or defense table. Illustrations of the types of computer-generated images developed for the Sacramento County Courthouse are provided on this page.

Ronald J. Budzinski, AIA, director of justice architecture for the firm of Hansen Lind Meyer, reminded conferees of Bill Lacy's caveat that courtroom participants often experience "extreme states of vulnerability." This suggests that architects should strive to provide, in the courtrooms they design, an optimum physical environment, a setting that will foster stability in judicial proceedings. If they succeed, judges and administrators are likely to weigh the design proposals they offer as carefully as jurists weigh trial evidence.

Technology

Technology can help make courtrooms and courthouses more secure from those who would harm judges, jurors, and staff or steal or sabotage sensitive court documents; more accessible to people with disabilities; more efficient and effective as a legal emporium serving bench and bar; and more of a school of justice for the people.

But as is so often the case in architecture, technology is no substitute for thoughtful, knowing planning and design or for designers willing to attempt to reconcile seemingly unreconcilable demands. Surprisingly, perhaps, this caveat was voiced more often by non-architects than by architects in the conference's sequence of panels on technology.

Security

Even the expert on terrorism—who said courtrooms make him uncomfortable because "you have to let everybody in" under circumstances that make it difficult to control them and "you are not paranoid if your ideology is that everybody is out to get you"—looked to the architect as the ultimate security provider. "The important thing is to have the security person involved in the planning from the beginning," said W. Douglas Fitzgerald, corporate director of security planning for Hansen Lind Meyer, an architecture, engineering, and planning firm. "It costs less that way."

Fitzgerald said that only a few years ago solutions to problems of court security were viewed in terms of technology. That orientation has changed, he said, and now more emphasis is placed on designing security into the courthouse and courtroom.

What are the principal design elements of secure courthouses and courtrooms? Panelists most often mentioned:

• Corridors of separation. The basis of personal security in the court setting is separation of judges, jurors, and prisoners, from one another and from the general courthouse population. Judges need protected parking in the courthouse and secure corridors to travel between car and chambers and between chambers and courtrooms. The same is true of jurors. And, because they can represent a security threat to judges and jurors, prisoners too must have segregated means of access to the courthouse and the courtroom.

All three classifications need to be segregated from the general public as they go about their roles in the judicial drama.

• Access control. Doug Fitzgerald's nightmare of a courthouse where "you have to let everyone in" is mitigated by controlling not only entrance to the courthouse but movement through it, a function enhanced by technology that ranges from the familiar closed-circuit television camera and identification cards that can unlock doors to scanners that can determine one's identity by reading fingerprints or a retina.

• Protection of sensitive court documents and information stored in computers. Judge Arlen Beam of the United States Court of Appeals for the Eighth Circuit raised the specter of impersonal violence to the judicial system by electronic spying. The growing dependence of the court on computerization of records and documents—including those sensitive in a trial or other action—makes it increasingly subject to invasion by computer hackers with evil intent. This, Judge Beam said, is a problem for the designer.

Just as technology has limits in assuring security, there are areas where design cannot go to protect judges and jurors, and those areas are outside the court environment. The impetus for greater attention to security issues, Judge Beam said, was the 1989 murder of a federal appeals court judge at his home in Alabama. It was buttressed by the increase in threats against federal judges from 125 nationwide in 1982 to 350 by the end of fiscal year 1991.

Don Horton, chief of the court security division of the U.S. Marshals Service, attributed the rise to "people angered by their involvement in federal litigation." Judge Beam said most judges would prefer to get along without any security arrangements whatsoever, but the Alabama murder has changed some minds. The Judicial Conference Committee on Judicial Security, which he chairs, now concerns itself with the security of judges in the court, off site, and in transit.

Judge Beam said that some judges, concerned about jurors' safety outside the courtroom, recess before it gets dark to minimize the danger of their getting to cars parked in inhospitable court environs.

Access by Persons With Disabilities

"Courthouses were built for the normal person," said Judge Richard S. Brown of the Court of Appeals of Wisconsin. What is normal, he asked? A 30-year-old right-handed man who doesn't have too much difficulty opening heavy doors, negotiating marble floors, seeing in dim light, mounting flights of stone entry steps, and climbing up into jury boxes or witness stands—or hearing testimony bouncing off the ceilings and walls of courtrooms designed more for majesty than good acoustics, Brown might have added. For he is deaf, one of the 43 million Americans who have some sort of disability and for whom the Americans with Disabilities Act (ADA) was enacted by Congress in 1992. The act, described by Judge Brown as neither conservative nor liberal in its approach but, rather, as problem-solving, requires that state and local government buildings, including courthouses, be accessible to persons with disabilities. (Covered by Uniform Federal Accessibility Standards, enacted earlier, federal buildings are exempted from ADA.)

More than 100 people turned out for the Friday morning session on accessibility, and they were treated to a powerful demonstration of the uses of computer-assisted technology in solving problems of access by people with disabilities and a subtle lesson in the importance of sensitivity and outreach by architects.

Looming at the right side of the meeting room was an enormous screen on which appeared, line by line, a real-time printed translation of everything the panel members said seconds after

In a computer-integrated courtroom, the court reporter's stenotype notes are translated and displayed on computer terminals within seconds of the words being spoken. Attorneys and the judge can search current or prior testimony, research case law, and perform other tasks while court is in sessions. The real-time quality of the display also helps hearing-impaired persons take part

Photographer: Unknown
© National Courts Reporters Association

they said it. The source was the familiar court reporter, seated at the foot of the speaker's dais, typing verbatim into a stenotype machine. The technology that produced this dramatic result was a program in a nearby computer that translates the symbols the reporter punched into his machine into words and punctuation. Transmitted in standard American English by the computer to an overhead projector, the words of the panelists were displayed, distinct and readable, on the big screen.

Judge Brown, who lost his hearing after he had learned to speak, used the audience's fascination with the real-

time translator to point out the importance of understanding the nature of the disabilities for which the architect must design barrier-free solutions.

Brown relies on real-time translation in his courtroom because English is his first language and he would find American Sign Language translators (like those one sees increasingly in televised political speeches) of little use. "ASL and English are two different languages and concepts of thinking," he said. By the same token, a person deaf since birth would find real time translation of little help and would need an ASL translator.

Such subtle but crucial shadings among disabilities pose a challenge to both architects, in designing courtrooms and courthouses, and court administrators, in the selection of technologies.

Carol Hatcher, deputy trial court administrator of Essex County, N.J., reflected on her experiences in the renovation of a 1902 courthouse to meet ADA standards and came up with a checklist:

1. Know the legislation and what you must and need not do under its terms.

2. Assemble a strong team to work with you, one that includes representatives of advocacy groups, like the Easter Seal Society or the Eastern Paralyzed Veterans Association. They have a wealth of information you can use and can be a tremendous resource. One such organization put together a survey group that guided Hatcher and her colleagues in their work.

3. Integrate accessibility into everything you do.

4. Survey your court building with a clear eye. People working in court buildings tend to think the buildings are more accessible than they are,

Hatcher said. Surveys reveal the shortcomings.

5. The ADA requires state and local public facilities to develop a multi-year plan for making the transition from inaccessible to accessible. This needs to be something you are thinking about on a regular basis, Hatcher said.

6. Don't be overwhelmed by the magnitude of the task.

7. Finally, once again, network with people in the community and in the communities of people with disabilities. They offer not only information but workable solutions as well.

If design repeatedly came to the fore more often than technology as the source of solutions to problems of accessibility, the potential of technology nevertheless had an assertive champion in the person of Judith Brentano, president of the National Court Reporters Association and an advocate of something she called Total Access Courtroom, a program of use to both the blind and the deaf and people without impairment, too.

In addition to real-time translation of proceedings, this program, she said, will offer:

• Computer software that permits the real-time transcript to be searched for specific references.

• Videotapes of the court proceedings that can use the real-time translation as captions or subtitles for what is being shown on the tape. The tape can be searched by computer for both sights and words.

• Computer software that permits integration of the video and text transcripts with other information in the court's case management data base. Because they can be stored on floppy computer disks, court-related data

become easier, quicker, and cheaper to share than has been traditional.

• Computer creation of Braille versions of court proceedings.

The key to all this technological progress is real-time translation and the machinery that accomplishes it, Brentano said. Only 26 of the country's courtrooms are set up to use it.

Technology in the Courtroom

Under the tutelage of Judge William G. Young, participants in the Friday afternoon session on courtroom technology sketched a view of the courtroom of the future that is firmly rooted in the judge's vision of the courtroom of the past and present.

The judge, who sits in Boston on the United States District Court for the District of Massachusetts, etched that vision simply:

"The courtroom is a place we come together to follow a process to resolve society's most intractable disputes. When we bring jurors into our courtrooms, that is the most vital expression of direct democracy in the United States today. Other than in town meetings or juries, all our democracy is representative. We hire the people who will govern us and make decisions. In the court, that is done by the people themselves."

This sublime objective ("We do not dispense justice in the courtroom; we reach out for it.") is approached through mundane activities that culminate in the courtroom and respond to four imperatives. One, in order for there to be a trial, a great deal of data must be gathered. Two, the data must be taught in the courtroom. Three, a record of both data and teaching must be kept. ("This is essential to our

concept of what is legal.") Four, people have a constitutional right to be there to witness the teaching of the data and its outcome.

How does 20th century technology fit into this almost Athenian vision of the courtroom as temple of justice cum school cum public theater? It fits very comfortably, and effectively as well, in the view of Judge Young and his co-panelists. Not only may technology permit the courtroom to continue filling its ancient functions in a more complex contemporary society with more and more intractable disputes to resolve. It may lend new power that will permit the courts to discharge those functions better than was ever possible before. Thus a new vision fuses with the old, and the concept of justice gains new vitality.

Judge Young illustrated the courtroom's function as classroom with a mesmerizing account of a presentation in 1974 by a lawyer representing the plaintiffs in a suit against an airline, one of the planes of which had crashed trying to land in dense fog at Logan Airport in Boston. His theory was that the crew had set the plane's altimeter incorrectly. To present it, the lawyer had sketched on four massive boards two lines of descent of the plane through the fog: one assuming a correct altimeter setting and showing the plane touching down safely on the runway; the other showing it descending too fast and striking the berm at the runway's end where, in fact, the crash occurred.

Reenacting the presentation, Young invited the audience to follow the fatal descent line in their minds while he repeated the words of the pilots as the plane descended, words taken from the cockpit recording found after the crash, a routine exchange among pilot, co-pilot, and tower, until—at the last second when he realizes he is flying into the ground—the pilot screams, "Christ!" and all sound goes dead.

The technology the lawyer employed in 1979 was foam core boards, felt pens, and audiotape. Having listened to Young's dramatic rendition of the last minute and 49 seconds of the lives of 94 human beings, it was not difficult to imagine how much more effective that presentation would have been as data-teaching if it could have employed the technology described to the audience by Judith H. Brentano, president of the National Court Reporters Association.

The courtroom of the future, as Brentano referred to it, was born in 1985 out of an effort to make it possible for deaf people to participate in courtroom proceedings. Her conception of the totally accessible courtroom uses the technology designed to assist hearing- and vision-impaired people to improve a range of judicial functions and procedures. The principal components of this technology are the computer and the familiar stenotype machine. Together, they produce the real-time transcript of court proceedings described earlier.

To the transcript stored in the computer can be added litigation support—depositions, case law, and notes—to be brought up as needed and displayed on computer or projector screens. "A digital data base can be integrated into the court's case management data base," Brentano said. "One file could encompass every element of a case," getting at one of the costliest items in court administration and architecture: records storage.

James McMillan, senior staff associate of the National Center for State Courts, pointed out that real-time reporting can be harnessed to data bases and both

functions can, in turn, be harnessed to computer simulations. Thus, it would be possible for witnesses to describe an event pertinent to a trial—for instance, an auto accident, an attempted murder, or an airliner crash—with the assistance of motion, color, perspective, and sound, and in a way that it would be nearly impossible to misunderstand or misinterpret.

Brentano's total-access courtroom answers three of the four requirements Judge Young set as a standard for a courtroom in which people reach for justice: it handles great amounts of data, it permits teaching that data effectively, and it keeps a meticulous record of the proceedings. But what about the fourth essential, the constitutional right of the public to be there?

In this regard, technology makes what may be its single greatest contribution in the form of television cameras in the courtroom, which bring trials to audiences larger than any courtroom could ever accommodate.

Steve Johnson, an Atlanta attorney who is executive producer of the Court TV channel, said his firm telecasts trials around the country for entertainment and commercial reasons and maintained that this does not detract from the educational power of the service. "Trials are great for examining issues," he said. "I would hope other media outlets would do the same thing." Between seven and eight million homes receive Court TV.

If the social implications of courtroom technology are large and breathtaking—anyone listening to Judge Young would be hard pressed to deny that they are—its practical implications for courtroom design and administration boil down to rather mundane choices.

One is between court reporters and audiotape. If you want a total access courtroom of Judith Brentano's envisioning, you go with the stenographer, and that is what Judge Young advocated. Perhaps the most difficult design decision flowing from this choice, a questioner suggested, is where to locate the court reporter's workstation.

If the judge is going to permit television cameras in court, the design implications are nearly nonexistent, Steve Johnson said. The camera is silent and has no lights on it, and the most common reaction of courtroom personnel newly exposed to it, he continued, is that it is forgotten within five minutes.

Because courtroom sound systems are not geared to television's requirement, television technicians prefer to install their own microphones, which are equally unobtrusive, he said. Threading and taping cable from the technical van into the courtroom does not create a pretty sight, but courthouse personnel soon become used to it. Perhaps the only design consideration is where to locate camera blinds. TV people prefer locations behind the judge and behind the jury.

Jim McMillan advised architects and administrators to build flexibility into their spaces and their systems to accommodate the changing networking capabilities, changing display capabilities, increasing computer power, and growing sophistication of the bar, jurors, and judges. In specific practical terms, what that requires is the provision of plenty of cable space during renovation or new construction.

The technological revolution is spreading slowly, courtroom by courtroom, Judge Young said, and this has disadvantages, one of which is that it costs more this way. "These things are vastly cheaper if they are in the design right from the outset."

Technology in the Courthouse

"In the end, I hope these buildings will still be recognizable as temples of justice," Judge Rya W. Zobel said as if in benediction at the close of the Friday session she chaired on courthouse technology.

Judge Zobel spoke both as a member of the United States District Court for the District of Massachusetts, which is having new court facilities built for it, and as someone who, like the 100-plus other people in the room, had heard some fairly unsettling things in the preceding hour and three-quarters about the likely effects of technology on the form and function of the courthouse in this country.

Whether these views of the future become reality seems to depend on how judges, court administrators, and designers respond to likely changes in the courthouse's seldom-mentioned role as an emporium of the legal business. Traditionally, the courthouse has been a quintessentially public institution, the hub of a legal enterprise that feeds on records, documents, books, and paper, "lots of paper," Judge Zobel said. Computers are changing that. It is now possible for lawyers to file briefs and other matters electronically. Computerized court records can be accessed electronically from outside the courthouse. Even the legal libraries can be browsed by computer. In other words, people in the legal business will not need to go to the courthouse as they have in the past.

What effect, Judge Zobel's panel asked, will this change have on courthouse traffic, staffing, and records management?

If one takes the last part of the question—records management—first, the response to the rest of the question is affected profoundly. The computer makes it possible to virtually eliminate paper as a significant factor in the management of court records. Mary Lu Holter, IBM's senior advisor for justice application, prophesied that "file cabinets are going to go away and probably books as well" and the records management system will generate paper only on demand. In the case of a large government—like Harris County, Tex. (Houston)—this would mean doing away with the 50,000-plus pages of mail it presently deals with each day.

The effect of such a development on the physical courthouse was not lost on Lawrence P. Webster, senior staff associate of the National Center for State Courts. "The layout of the courthouse today is based on the paper flow," he said. "With imaging (computer storage of records), that doesn't have to happen any more. It means we are not physically bound."

And that is precisely what bothered some of the panelists and the audience members alike. Being physically bound to the legal emporium as well as the temple of justice produces interactions that benefit the agencies of justice and the citizenry.

For example: Jackie Busse of Gray's Harbor Superior Court in Montesanto, Wash., objected that, "the people who elected us don't want to use this technology. They want to have to do directly with us."

Judge Zobel said that recorded depositions are not catching on with lawyers because this basically technological process lacks the interaction of a courtroom proceeding.

Another example: William Butler, deputy court administrator for Prince George's County, Md., who helped build the new county courthouse in Upper Marlboro, tried to slow the panel's developing consensus that reduced courthouse traffic means less space that needs to be devoted to hallways. He reminded the audience that not everybody who does business with the court is rich enough to have a computer.

At least one member of the audience seemed agitated by Judge Zobel's musing that, "We might be handling civil rights actions from prisoners by television." What about the right of the accused to face the accuser, he asked. Judge Zobel replied that this form of technology could be employed only in administrative actions and that the right of confrontation could not be abridged.

But she, too, seemed concerned about the prospect of peopleless courthouses. "The courthouses will have to remain open for some time," she said. "So, designers, please leave amenities for the public."

The effects of technology on courthouse staffing have not been entirely positive, it appears. "We have not reduced the numbers of people who work in the courts," Judge Zobel said. "But we have changed the kinds of skills that are employed there." Prince George's County's Butler agreed. "As we bring all this technology into court, we need technologists to run it," a prospect he made clear is not entirely congenial to him.

Citing evidence that computers free staff people for doing more work, one attendee questioned why resistance to computerization persists. Judge Zobel replied, "It is not clear that we need all the information they produce by doing more work. Part of the problem is the technology. Back in the day of the quill pen, you got one-page briefs. Briefs got longer with the introduction of the fountain pen, longer still with the typewriter, and, now, longer still with the computer."

Butler ticked off a long list of intensely practical considerations for people involved in designing and overseeing design of courthouses. The special requirements of modems, bar scanners, wall-less workstations, pre-selected lighting environments and lighting programs, and sound systems all seemed to require increased ventilation. "Our buildings are becoming giant cable trays," he said, and consultants and subcontractors elbow one another for preferred position of their cables in those trays.

The saving grace, he suggested, is that the principal demand that technology makes on design at the most rudimentary level is for cable space. Beyond that, he advised, "A facilities designer cannot be 100 percent correct. Create art and conceal all the gizmos."

MANAGEMENT

Project Team

Glenn Gauger, AIA, a principal of Sverdrup Corp., traced the traditional system of delivering design and construction services to the master builders of the Middle Ages who provided what in today's parlance might be called the one-stop shop of service delivery. In the traditional system, the architect has assumed a clearinghouse function, supplying information and guidance to all the other major players: user, owner, engineer, and contractor.

But times are changing, and so are the roles of many of the players. Gauger, whose office in St. Louis participates in many of the emerging patterns of partnership, gave an overview of today's classic delivery systems.

Gauger described some of the forces of change: The industry is more fragmented and complex. More consultants are providing a broader range of services. Subcontractors and material providers have become highly specialized. When cost overruns and delays proliferate, the construction project can become a battleground, with participants, through their lawyers, contending they have suffered financial harm.

Construction Management

This problem has led many owners to look to different delivery methods, Gauger said. These are classified generally under the rubric of construction management. Noting that this term means many things to many people, Gauger provided this definition: "Construction management (CM) is a

project delivery method that takes a systematic approach to planning and monitoring the cost, schedule, and quality of construction projects."

The roles of the owner, contractor, and construction manager may change in different project-delivery scenarios. In the first departure from the traditional approach, which Gauger called the "Agency CM Organization," the construction manager, like the architect, acts as an agent of the owner. This method, CM in its purest form, is typically used in public projects, particularly those at the county level.

In the next variation, commonly called the "At Risk CM Organization," the CM takes responsibility for costs but still acts in an agent's role. Under some circumstances he or she acts as an independent contractor. This sometimes creates confusion because as the design develops and costs are fixed the CM acts in partnership with the owner, assuming a different mind-set.

In the third variation, the architect, the engineer, and the construction manager start to come together as one contractual entity. This is often called the extended-service CM organization. Typically, in this form the concept for the building is developed by others and the CM team completes the design and construction for a guaranteed price.

In a fourth variation, a design/construction organization provides total design, construction, and program management, almost coming full circle to the medieval master builder concept. The program manager, or design/builder,

contracts directly with the owner to provide all services, guaranteeing cost and adherence to schedule. He or she often provides the mechanism for funding the project through financial advisors or may actually take title to the completed project and lease it back to the agency.

Legislation Lags Behind Industry Practices

Gauger issued some caveats. The operation of these systems can run afoul of laws and regulatory practices of some states, he warned, because state legislation has not kept pace with the evolution of the industry. He also listed advantages and disadvantages of each system (shown on the accompanying tables).

"I don't advocate one form or the other," Gauger said, "but my

---

Advantages and disadvantages of major project-delivery systems, as listed by Glenn Gauger, AIA, of Sverdrup Corporation.

Traditional

Advantages:

- The architect is an advocate for design intent.
- The project investment is limited to A/E fees.
- The owner selects the A/E on the basis of ability.

Disadvantages:

- There is a shift in prime management responsibilities at construction.
- Control over project costs is limited.
- Contractors are often selected on the basis of low bid rather than management abilities.
- The design/bid/construction cycle is longer.

Agency CM

Advantages:

- Competitive bidding of prime contracts.
- The owner selects the CM on the basis of ability.
- The owner has an expert construction advocate.
- Construction input is provided early during the design phases.
- A system of checks and balances is provided.
- Controlled competitive fast-tracking can be used.
- There is focused management of the owner's risks.
- Decision making is quick and accurate.

Disadvantages:

- The owner is most at risk for ultimate construction cost.
- The owner retains ultimate responsibility for design quality, cost, and schedule.
- The CM has no real clout to resolve design/construction issues but serves only as mediator.

Extended-services CM Organization

Advantages:

- Single-source responsibility for design and construction management.
- CM can guarantee fee for design and CM services.
- CM could hold subcontracts.

Disadvantages:

- Many CM firms do not have in-house design capability.
- There is no objective A/E to focus on design issues.
- Procurement laws may prohibit this process in certain jurisdictions.

Design/Construction Organization

Advantages:

- Single-source responsibility for design and construction.
- CM can guarantee cost for design and construction.

Disadvantages:

- Most construction firms do not have in-house design capability.
- There is no objective A/E to focus on design issues.
- Procurement laws may be prohibited in certain jurisdictions.

Charleston Federal Courthouse, Charleston, W.Va.

Photographer: Brian Nolan
Model: Richard Tenguerian
© Skidmore Owings & Merrill,
New York, N.Y.

experience has been that the more focused the responsibility, the more focused the results; the more complex the project and schedule become, the more critical the communications become between the participants.

"Properly managed, any one of these mechanisms can yield a successful project. For a courthouse in Missouri, for which our firm was project manager under the design construction model, we guaranteed the construction price at completion of the programming stage."

That jurisdiction, Gauger explained, had a history of failed referendums and large cost overruns. Hence, the county lacked the credibility needed to obtain financing. With the early guarantee, the county was able to gain voter approval of a sales tax referendum and, because the bondholder had assurances the project would be delivered as represented, it was able to sell the bonds at good rates.

How CM Techniques Apply to Three Courthouses

Gary Haney, AIA, of the New York office of Skidmore, Owings and Merrill, described the effect on design of three federal courthouse projects his firm is designing in which management techniques discussed by Gauger were used. Whatever the management pattern, Haney said, communication of decision making is perhaps the single most important factor.

In the design and development of a 350,000-square-foot courthouse with 12 courtrooms in Charleston, W.Va., a straightforward contract with GSA provides for a traditional relationship between the architect and engineers and the court family that will occupy the building.

A design/build team is supervising design and construction of a much smaller federal courthouse in White Plains, N.Y. The project defies

White Plains Federal Courthouse, White Plains, N.Y.

Brooklyn Federal Courthouse, Brooklyn, N.Y.

Gauger's rule of thumb, which suggests that the design/build scenario is more appropriate for larger projects, which generally use repetitive processes. The bulk (five volumes) required to outline the White Plains program attests to the complexity of the project.

"The relationship between the architect and the end user is more distant than in the traditional process," Gauger said. "In the Brooklyn federal building, the largest of the projects, a developer was brought in by the owner of the site. We were hired as part of a developer team by the owner who is providing the building to the GSA, which will provide it to the court family. Here the architect becomes even more distant from the end user. As the players increase in number, my job becomes more and more complicated."

Haney emphasized again the importance of communication. Displaying a diagram depicting a complicated relationship of owners, users, consultants, and other participants, he described a dilemma often faced by the architect: "Who is my client? You feel compelled to work directly with the end user. This is the person who is going to occupy your building. However, you cannot meet directly with them in some of these systems without having the person who is going to pay for the building present. The point here is that communication between these groups is absolutely critical. What works best for architects, is that a single point of contact be identified for each group—a person with the ability and authority to provide direction or at least find answers for you quickly."

The View From the Bench

"I'm here because I'm the flesh and blood version of the charts, the outlines, and the plans," said Judge Paul F. Sheridan of Virginia's 17th Judicial District. He thus launched into a firsthand, often highly personal, account of the planning, programming, and early stages of construction of a courthouse that commands a view of the Washington, D.C., Mall and the national Capitol from a site adjoining Arlington National Cemetery.

"One of the pleasures of being a judge," said Sheridan, "is that you can tell people when the conversation is over. Yet this process, which is so vital, challenges judges to use their skills for listening and participation to a far greater degree than our training and oath of office usually require us to do."

His advice, dispensed alternately to architects and the judicial community, was drawn from his experiences in coordinating the decisions made by the Arlington County court's four judges in planning the $27 million, 283,000-square-foot courthouse, now under construction. Even though it has one of the highest levels of income in the state, the urban-suburban county, across the Potomac River from Washington, D.C., has a high crime rate. The 15-story courthouse will replace a seven-story structure completed in 1960.

Judge Sheridan did not purport to provide conference participants with precise answers to their design and construction problems, but he certainly offered them questions. In determining the size of courtrooms, he suggested asking: "How many bodies will come into this courtroom? How many hours a day do the bodies stay there? Can docketing (scheduling) issues take care

Arlington County Courthouse/Police Facility Model, Arlington, Va.

Photographer: Unknown
© Hansen Lind Meyer, Reston, Va.

of things we can't accomplish physically? If you have 300 people in a room for 30 minutes while you divide up the docket, why don't you change the docketing system? This is outside the realm of design; it's a matter for judges to resolve.

"You've got to know how a court is run," declared Sheridan as a prelude to another battery of questions. "Do the judges run individual dockets? In the general docket, do the judges all share the same kind of cases on a rotating basis? How do the papers get from the files to the court? Instead of having a court reporter taking a verbatim record, are we going to an electronic system and, if so, where do operators place their equipment?"

Security was a major concern for Sheridan and his fellow judges, perhaps largely because of the lack of it in the existing Arlington County courthouse. "You can now can walk up to my desk with a shotgun," he said. "If you think security is not significant, consider the fact that during August my children had sheriffs' protection because of an explicit death threat. These things gain your attention. Security will be real to the judges with whom you work."

The Arlington County judges are also concerned about the security of juries. "Our juries in Virginia don't just say 'guilty,' they set the sentence at the same time. Our jurors then leave the courtroom, get on the elevator, and join the defendant's family and go down to the parking lot. The jurors mingle with the beloved of the guy they just put in prison for 20 years."

While making provisions for security, the Arlington jurists sought to avoid building a "frightening citadel," Sheridan said. "The visual impact on the public should say the court is not the police, not the same as the prosecutor," even though these entities and the sheriff's office will be quartered in the same building. The building will have a clear demarcation of entrances for each of these governmental units to enhance the public perception that there is a clear distinction between their functions and those of the courts.

Like other speakers, Judge Sheridan advocates visiting other court facilities, not just as a passive observer of the courtrooms and the chambers. And, of course, he counseled, go prepared with questions.

"Don't just sit in the back of the courtroom. Sit in the holding cell. Can a prisoner in the holding cell scream loudly enough to be heard in the courtroom? If you have a disruptive prisoner you want to put in another room, is that person still going to disrupt the trial because the heating and air conditioning ducts allow the voice of the screamer to be heard in the courtroom?" The question was prompted by just such an occurrence when Sheridan and his associates visited a courthouse in Chesterfield County, Va.

Architect Selection

The three key groups involved in selection of an architect to design a courthouse—the architect, the judiciary, and the building's managers—approach the project from three distinct perspectives. How well the courthouse looks and functions for its initial users

and generations of their successors depends, in the consensus of three panelists, on how successfully these perspectives are reconciled in the selection process.

Edward Feiner, chief architect of GSA, provided insight on the distinctly different calculations of the prime players in the decision process:

"The architect is thinking: 'How can I get the job?' The judiciary wants to know how to get the best functional courthouse that meets its goals and objectives. As government managers, we in GSA are interested in getting an excellent building but also in a process that will enable us to get it built within budget and on schedule."

In view of these priorities, often overlapping but viewed somewhat differently by each beholder, what should guide judges and their administrative colleagues in selecting an architect? How can architects and their teams of associates and consultants present their abilities and their visions of the planned courthouse in the best light?

Feiner, Judge Douglas P. Woodlock, of the United States District Court of the District of Massachusetts, and architect Michael Frawley, AIA, each drew on extensive experience in exploring these and a range of related questions from their own perspectives. Each had advice to offer architects competing for commissions and for the judges and administrators who evaluate their presentations.

The Four Cs

Feiner, who manages a federal construction program with $10 billion worth of work in progress, listed attributes he feels would give architecture firms an edge in competing. He called them the four Cs: Competence,

consistency, client concern, and creativity. Judge Woodlock, who chairs the space and facilities committee in his judicial district and serves on that committee's counterpart for the United States Judicial Conference, discussed the selection process under the rubric of integrity, education, and engagement. In a methodical outline for architect selection, Frawley, a designer in the Orlando, Fla., office of Hansen Lind Meyer, raised many of the same points and identified a less tangible element, the "comfort factor." He explained: "The architect chosen should be a person (or firm) in whom there can be a relationship of absolute confidence and trust; one with whom a certain rapport is established at the outset."

In explaining how the four Cs should be applied, Feiner emphasized that architect selection is a multi-stage process guided by federal procurement policy. This policy is spelled out in the Brooks Act, a landmark federal law for the architectural and engineering professions. In the first stage of the process, GSA must assure that the process will be competitive by preparing a slate of the most highly qualified architecture firms for any given project. This pre-selection step, he explained, might require a review of all the firms in a sparsely populated Western state, while a search of firms in two square blocks of Manhattan or San Francisco might yield an adequate slate of competitors. All the firms surviving this agency screening process will possess the first two Cs: competence and consistency.

The next stage of the selection process will determine which of the contending firms exhibit the remaining two Cs—client concern and creativity. Identifying these qualities is one of the challenges for the selection panel.

The Supreme Court of the United States, Washington, D.C.

Photographer: Unknown
© Collection, Supreme Court Historical Society, Washington, D.C.

Ideally, Feiner said, this group should be a mix, including technical experts, peers of the designers to be considered, people with managerial backgrounds, and users—in the case of courthouses, judges, and administrative officers. After a series of intensive interviews with principals of the competing architecture firms and, in some cases, after visits to their offices and sites of buildings they have completed, this panel chooses a firm to design the building and negotiates a fee for its services.

All three conference panelists emphasized the importance of the interviews the selection group must conduct with the competing architecture firms. To architects who, typically, have less than two hours to make a presentation for what might be their firm's most significant work in a quarter century, Feiner emphasized: "You have to be able to communicate quickly, eloquently, and elegantly. You get only a few sound

bites to put your points across. Choose them very carefully." By the same token, he said, members of the selection panel must listen carefully to be able to sort out the significance of these succinct communications. The selection panel, Feiner suggested, might prepare for its encounter with the architects by asking itself a basic question: "What do we really want in this building? Do we want something classical or something cutting edge? You will be unhappy if you select an architect who is into Russian deconstructivism if your vision of your new courthouse is the United States Supreme Court building."

Feiner, who critiques designs of all federal buildings, ranging from courthouses to border stations, emphasized that "this [interviewing] is the part of the process that deals with people. The problems the selection panel faces cannot can be solved by a mathematical equation or by throwing a mass

of data into a computer to be electronically analyzed. A small group of people must absorb a phenomenal amount of information in visual and tabular form and then make a decision."

Feiner provided some dos and don'ts for architects appearing before selection panels:

• The interview should not be a regurgitation of the standard government Forms 254 and 255.

• It is not a true or false test to reveal whether you are a post-modernist or a post-classicist.

• It is not a time to parade every consultant on the team and give them each five minutes to offer assurances, for example, that your structure will not fall down or will respond correctly to changes in the thermostat.

• Provide some insight about the firm's incipient vision of the project, even some visual evidence of this vision. This doesn't mean offering a solution to the program or saying, "Here is the design for your courthouse." But the firm's designers should demonstrate that they have thought specifically about the project and can show examples of previous work applicable to it.

Feiner also offered some guidance to the jurists and administrators:

• Listen to the architects. Probe their philosophies, their attitudes, their sensitivity, and thought processes. Look for sincerity and commitment.

• Expecting a firm's signature designer or a senior partner to spend full time on your project, although desirable, may not be realistic. Hence, try to determine what kind of commitment the firm's whole team is prepared to make to your project.

• Visit offices of competing architecture firms and, when it is feasible, examine examples of recently completed work of the competing firms.

"The truth is," Feiner reiterated, "there is no guaranteed solution or mathematical equation that gives you the right selection. It's not a science. It is an art."

Michael Frawley summarized a presentation that could serve as a manual for architect selection. He outlined activities typical to the selection method most widely used for public projects, discussed professionally accepted factors for evaluating architects, and provided a protocol to clients for carrying out the process.

Although a business-like approach to the subject, Frawley's treatise was laced with practical advice for both architects and clients. For example:

• "On many court projects, it is common to find associations of firms rather than one firm. In that instance, it is important to determine how the firms propose to work together. Ascertain the proposed division of responsibilities, the availability of expertise as appropriate, and the adequacy of the proposed project logistics."

• "Recognize that there is no correlation between an architect's ability and an architect's ability to speak. You are hiring an architect, not an orator."

Integrity, Education, and Engagement

To underscore the importance of integrity in the architect selection process, Judge Woodlock prefaced his discussion with the story of the selection of an accountant in the 1980s by the CEO of a major company bent on expanding his horizons and attracting investors. To each of three accountants,

this executive asked a single question: "How much is 2 + 2?" The first two gave the obvious answer, but the third replied with a question of his own: "How much you want it to be?"

"That selection process, I suggest to you, is somewhat self-defeating in cases in which judges are involved," Judge Woodlock said. "There is an immense concern for the integrity of the professional with whom you are dealing, and the effort to coddle, warm up to, or snuggle—at least the judicial participants, and I think all participants—is not likely to be successful.

"I have in mind a recent architectural selection process involving a federal court in which a judge who had no particular predispositions toward the architectural style he would like to see employed for his courthouse turned to a very famous architect and said: 'You know, every one of your buildings seems to be white and modern.' The arrayed consultants around the architect were atwitter, concerned that he would lose this competition by saying something other than, 'What do you want 2 + 2 to be?' The architect looked directly at the judge and said, 'That's exactly right. If you hire me you will get a white and modern building?'

"After the selection process I remember talking to some of the consultants who thought that was the worst possible answer. Of course, it was the best because the judge involved said that was the most significant thing that had been said in the interview. It was someone speaking to him about the integrity of his professional engagement. That single factor more than any other is one that is going to draw at least the judiciary, including judges, to consider carefully the presentations made by a team."

Judge Woodlock discussed lessons he and his court colleagues learned in a tour of buildings of architects on the short list for the new Boston federal courthouse, now in late stages of programming. Following an itinerary arranged by consultant Bill Lacy, the team examined, among others outside the Boston area, buildings in New York designed by Cesar Pelli and Skidmore, Owings and Merrill; the Becton-Dickenson corporate headquarters in suburban New Jersey by Kallmann, McKinnel and Wood; the work of Robert Venturi at Princeton University; Commerce Square by Harry Cobb in Philadelphia, and Canada's National Gallery of Art by Moshe Safdie.

"That process," Woodlock said, "was education. That is what judges do for a living. They are educated by other people. And if you, as an architect, are willing to understand and attempt to educate and buy into what is probably the single characteristic of a judicial officer—a kind of relentless self-improvement, a desire to learn more about what is going on around him or her to make reasoned judgments—then you are going to have a leg up in the selection process."

Judge Woodlock said he, Chief Judge Stephen Breyer of the United States Court of Appeals in Boston, and others involved in selecting an architect for the new courthouse there determined that interviews in that process would not be cluttered by routine recitations of consultants. Instead, he said, they were "intensive discussion of the architecture firms' design philosophy, of what they thought they were doing with a courthouse, what they thought they could bring to bear on the project that justified building the most important building that would be built in the city of Boston for the next quarter century at the very least."

By the same token, he said, "it is exceptionally important that architects engage the judges and others involved in the selection process in understanding that what they are doing is the most important thing that someone can do with a building in their community in the same period."

"It is disappointing when judicial members of a selection panel are not engaged or ask rote questions," Judge Woodlock said. "I think most judges I am familiar with understand the importance of being fully engaged and recognize that if they are not, the building won't function properly. More than that, it will not be an icon but an eyesore. Chief Judge Breyer once said during a selection process, 'Twenty years from now nobody is going to remember any of the opinions we wrote, but they are going to look at that building and are either going to blame us or thank us, and we going to have to determine which one it is going to be by being actively engaged.'

Interviews can be most effective, Judge Woodlock suggested when this engagement is reciprocated by an architect who "is interested, determined, and understands the needs of the judiciary and is willing to engage in a dialectic— a dialectic that might involve saying, 'If you get me it will be white and modern,' but at the same time involve a willingness to respond to the critiques that are provided by the judge himself or herself."

Consider, Judge Woodlock said, the integrity, education, and engagement provided by the description of courthouse design and construction in William Faulkner's Requiem for a Nun:

…[T]he architect had told them [citizens of Faulkner's fictional Yoknapatawpha County] they had no money to buy bad taste with, nor even anything from which to copy what bad taste might still have been within their compass.

The novelist concluded this passage with an elegy to the courthouse that was finally created:

The courthouse was theirs bigger than any because it was the sum of all. And it left them with something like humility as if they were realizing, or for the first moment at least capable of realizing, and believing that all men, including themselves, were a little better, purer maybe even, than they had thought, expected, or needed to be.

"That's what ultimately all of us want," Woodlock said. "We want to be engaged in a selection process that is going to give us people of integrity who in an adversarial climate will work with us to build a great courthouse, people who are going to educate us because we are going to be spending a lot of time and we shouldn't do it stupidly, and people who are going to engage us in a way we should be engaged in this great public enterprise."

Planning the 100-Year Courthouse

"We have seen the future and it closely resembles the past." This succinct statement captured much of the sentiment expressed by a panel of architects and planners of judicial facilities as they outlined their vision of the courthouse of the next century. Moderator Geoff Gallas, executive administrator of the First Judicial District of Pennsylvania, challenged representatives of both disciplines to draw on their analytical data, their professional experience, and their imagination to project the future needs of the judicial process and to suggest how those needs might realistically be met.

The panelists agreed that tomorrow's courthouses must be made adaptable to potential changes—indeed to changes already taking place—in techniques of dispute resolution and technology. But none was ready to embrace wholeheartedly the "virtual courthouse" or systems in which the electronic dispensation of justice would replace the face-to-face judicial process in important criminal or civil procedures.

The discussion ranged over such issues as the validity of projecting statistical techniques in gauging courthouse needs, the ratio of chambers to courtrooms, the impact of changing demographic and ethnic patterns on the judicial process, the merits of multiple-use facilities, the value of preserving symbolism, and the need to tie courthouse planning to city and metropolitan area planning.

Repeatedly, however, the discussion took a "back to the future," tack, largely through the prodding of Gallas, who kept posing such questions as:

"Are we looking toward building smaller, more flexible, smarter buildings, even in major metropolitan areas, because of advances in communications? Is that the future of courthouse design or are we going to build, at least in the urban areas, the mega courthouse where we house all our judicial officers?"

"How the technological explosion will affect the judicial process is a great imponderable at this moment," replied Michael Thomas, a principal in Justice Planning Associates. "I'm not sure, but I find myself wondering if the courthouse is going to change from public assembly place, as it is now, to a giant studio. The idea of a judge at a console is out there in the wings. It would be possible to conceive of courtrooms redistributed in the community. Judges, instead of going to their respective courtrooms on foot or in cars, might go to them electronically."

Gallas kept pressing. "Can you see yourself being called into a community as a consultant and saying: 'What you need is three courthouses with four judges in each location and facilities to move voice and image back and forth between those or between the parties as an alternative approach.'"

"I'm not sure its good to impose electronic media on the concept of individual justice," said Dan Wiley. "But I think its happening and we have to give consideration to the facilities that will result." He noted that telephone conferences among participants in the judicial process are common and facilities are linked by video.

F. Michael Wong, FAIA, of Space Management Consultants, reminded the panelists that building mega courthouses won't preclude the dispersion of judicial facilities throughout the community. "In Los Angeles," he said, "there are court service centers. They might be in shopping malls or in small buildings. Those service centers handle traffic cases, small claims, perhaps some family disputes."

A willingness to compromise with an inevitable tide of communications techniques emerged.

"Two issues are actually involved here," Thomas insisted. "Technology is only one of them, and that's not the hard one. We can divide the case types. Limited-jurisdiction courts seem to work well in satellite facilities. . . . It would be possible now or shortly in the future to have criminal or civil trials at any level conducted with the judge in

an office and with jury at their homes linking in on closed circuit television or through holographic display, with the attorneys in individual offices. The more fundamental question is not, 'Will the technology be available?' but 'Will the court system choose to use it?' or 'Is it a good thing to do?'

"We've heard a lot in the last two days about the symbolism of the court and judicial system. I think we would be losing a great deal if we accepted the kind of litigation model I just posed. I think it could work very well for certain types of cases, but in others people do need that day in court to leave psychologically satisfied that they have received justice."

Jordan Gruzen, FAIA, concurred. "We are going to have an increasing technology and a peeling away of those proceedings like traffic court and many other levels in which presence is not essential," he said. "But for the real life and death issues, the criminal issues, where you want to look into the eyes and see that subtlety of movement, the flinching of an eye that perhaps the television camera won't pick up—this is a human experience that is not going to be replaced by the electronic substitute."

These panelists paid their respects, as did other conference participants to the historical courthouse, the courthouse as the center of the community, the preeminent civic symbol, the meeting place, the place where citizens went for news and even, on occasion, for entertainment. For most of these purposes it has been replaced now by media coverage and sporting events. As a result, said Michael Thomas, "it has been reduced to a place of business. The driving force has been increasing caseloads and the need to be more

efficient in the timely resolution of disputes.

"We are now getting back into a situation where the very cost of building a courthouse makes us want to make it a better investment for the community. So we want to involve the community more in the daily function of the court and not lose that thread of cultural and legal continuity. I think we see in Boston a wonderful example of trying to blend the building into the landscape of the city so that it can be a place of public pleasure as well as a place of business. But for the average county or city, greater public involvement may come down to trying to bring in civic groups and make double use of spaces such as having jury assembly areas serve as meeting places in the evening."

Gallas was unwilling to abandon the gadfly role. "Can any of you," he asked, "imagine the electronic courthouse literally. We can see images of the participants. You can wear a suit or you can wear your flip-flops with no shirt. We could present electronically the majesty of justice, the symbol of the judge. Through virtual reality you could project court participants into the conventional courthouse. The judge could appear at eye level to Wilt Chamberlain or Willie Shoemaker. Is there any possibility that's what the courthouse is going to be in 100 years?"

"There are certain procedures that, in all likelihood, will be handled that way increasingly," Thomas conceded. "There are other types of procedures, life and death matters, major civil cases, and even hotly contested domestic cases, where the personal interaction and the symbolism of coming together with the court as the ultimate arbiter in an elevated position is going to be necessary. We live with symbolism and it has an important effect on our everyday psychological life. I think to move to a model that ignores that basic human need is probably not appropriate."

"I think you will get 100 percent consensus for that," said Walter Sobel, FAIA, of Walter Sobel and Associates.

The panelists also discussed the reliability of statistical tools that are frequently used for forecasting courthouse needs. They agreed that it is necessary to use such techniques as regression analysis and historic trend analysis but cautioned that results from these analyses must be applied with sound judgment.

Good forecasting, Michael Thomas contended, requires application of both science and art. "The science aspect," he suggested, "involves an analysis of trends. The art part of it is the exercise of judgment in the likelihood that future trends will tend to mirror past trends and for that you have to have some understanding and some insight into the dynamics of the system."

Thomas and fellow panelists cautioned against projecting trends too far into the future. Jordan Gruzen cited dynamic changes in the South Bronx as a case in point. "In a short time," he noted, "it changed from an extremely affluent, stable middle class community with a low crime rate to a low income, high-crime minority area. If one had tried to make a 25-year projection, it would have been totally meaningless. Therefore you need to integrate not only court statistics, but city planning issues into forecasting. You need to know what has happened to immigration laws, what is happening with dynamics of the city plan, the county plan, and to see other major

changes that could throw statistics out the window."

Gallas opened a discussion of the optimum ratio of courtrooms to chambers by asking: "Is the future one-judge, one-courtroom?" The consensus: probably not.

"Over the last 10 years we have been trying, particularly in the county and state court system, to develop multiple-use facilities, allocating more chambers than courtrooms, in anticipation in the future of more flexible facilities for the justice system," said Michael Wong. "We are designing judges chambers to courtrooms in the ratio between 11-13 chambers for 10 courtrooms.

The ratio of judges to courtrooms is only one aspects of courthouse planning that is in flux, Gruzen suggested. "The implication in the Boston example is that things are coming into the building both through the judges initiative and the community's initiative, which were never found in courthouses before: daycare centers, art galleries, educational facilities, allowing school children to come in and be educated in justice, recreation centers, witness holding areas—things we don't find in the old courthouses. How we plan for the flexibility is one of the key elements—the flexibility to accept these changing ratios in the core and also accept these peripheral facilities.

In summary remarks all the panelists paid tribute to symbolism.

Said Gruzen, "Society needs its icons, its monuments. As long as there is going to be a courthouse, the courthouse has to represent the highest aspirations of our society in the form of architecture and that form of architecture has got to be expressive, symbolic of this cradle of justice and that ideal

that has been with us through the centuries is not something that is suddenly going to disappear through electronics. The search must continue for evolving forms that symbolize those high aspiration of society and even if they must be shrunken elements because of economic constraints."

Financing the Courthouse

Robert Tobin, staff attorney and management consultant of the National Center for State Courts, faced a small group of conferees at the end of a day replete with discussion of such lofty matters as image, symbolism, iconography; deliberations about optimum positions for the bench, jury box, and witness stand; and colloquies between advocates of natural light and defenders of windowless, controlled environments.

"The new courthouse is a relative rarity," Tobin's told this group, primed to return to their communities to help build a courthouse that might last up to 100 years.

He acknowledged that new construction "is the first thing that comes to mind" when the subject of financing court facilities arises. But as a prelude to discussing financing he offered a bleak assessment of the many, and often mundane, claims made on dollars allocated for the judiciary.

"Just day-to-day operating costs are now a problem," Tobin said. "A lot of courthouses are literally falling down. With some notable exceptions, the court plant is aging. Maintenance, custodial services, insurance, and utilities are basic costs. The biggie now is security. I'm not speaking about security provided for transportation of prisoners or bailiffs' salaries, but security for the building as a whole. This has kicked up the cost of operations significantly in court after court. It is draining what little resources are available for renovation or construction.

Financing Renovation

"Renovation is probably the major capital expenditure most courts make. Most courthouses are in a constant state of renovation. The addition of new judges requires capital expenditures on a greater scale than initial construction. Widespread regard for the majesty of justice notwithstanding, when it comes to financing, courthouses in most states "are no different from other public buildings," Tobin said. "There is," he added, "court-specific financing in certain states. But generally speaking, the courts have to deal with the financing mechanisms that affect any public agency."

It is important to define what we mean by a court facility," said Tobin, noting some serious proposals a few years ago to build regional facilities that encountered resistance for legal, traditional, and political reasons. "What's going on now," he said, "is a reverse trend. There is great deal of decentralization under way, for a variety of reasons, including topography, climate, or populations change. You may find that officials of a county with two population centers, both with strong bars, maintain courthouses in different parts of the county. You are seeing terrific distribution of court facilities in Florida, where there are large population concentrations. A recent study showed that Pinellas County has 13 court facilities, some in the northern part of the county, some between Clearwater and St. Petersburg, and a separate criminal complex adjoining the county jail."

Tobin noted that not every court facility is the setting for criminal or civil trials. Some actually function as centers for social or health programs or as arbitration facilities. "The Circuit Court of Cook County has a psychiatric Institute in its budget," he said. "You'll find some courts administering domestic violence centers."

Diverse Financing Instruments

Focusing on trial courts as the core of his review of financing, Tobin described a broad array of arrangements.

"Thirty states pay operational costs of their trial courts, but only 10 finance court facilities. Even among the 10 states that finance facilities, some of them may not take title to the building. Massachusetts gives counties an option. A county may turn over title to the state, in which case the state assumes debt service and all the cost of the building. But if a county wants to keep title, it has to meet certain specifications. In some of the 10 states the only means of state payment is by reimbursement to the county."

Tobin listed the following financing instruments in common use:

• Revolving funds. Jurisdictions can draw on these funds to facilitate design and pay a range of front-end costs. These funds are sometimes replenished from bond funds, from appropriations, and, increasingly, from earmarked fees.

• Lines of credit. These are often used for front-end costs and occasionally for renovation and the funds advanced are paid back from capital funds.

• State and county general funds. Small construction, particularly renovation, may be financed in this way.

• Facility funds. These funds are accumulated from by court costs,

usually from civil cases, where fees are collected up front. Among states authorizing such funds are California, North Carolina, Maine, and Florida.

• Revenue bonds and authorities. These can be general public authorities, state or local. Some states have established authorities or commissions for a particular construction project; the commission goes out of existence after the revenue bonds are retired, typically in 20 years. Alabama, on the other hand, established a permanent judicial building authority for appellate court construction. Usually courts rely on a public authority that finances other public entities. Courts can also tie into state capital funds or local capital improvement plans, which often means participating in lengthy programming processes. Because courts are often hit suddenly with legislative mandates to expand quickly, they may find this a cumbersome process. Connecticut relies heavily on leasing to provide space for its courts.

Recognizing the crumbling condition of court facilities in New York, the legislature permitted an agency established to finance college dormitories to provide funds to build and renovate courthouses.

Some states make grants to courts. Typically, these are used for such facilities as juvenile detention centers, family-counseling centers, and community-based corrections facilities. Finally, the public-private partnership, a device seized eagerly by public agencies since the early 1980s to stretch scarce revenue, is providing unfamiliar venues for selected judicial procedures. "Private developers are putting outreach court facilities—not criminal facilities—in some of their developments," Tobin said.

Outlook for Funding Federal Court Facilities

John Callahan, deputy staff director of the Senate Budget Committee, discussed the outlook for funds to build and renovate federal court facilities. "We think there will be renewed emphasis on an economic stimulus package in the 103rd Congress," said Callahan, speaking a few days before the election of Bill Clinton as president. He noted that Clinton had made investment in infrastructure one of the centerpieces of his campaign.

"If we do have an economic stimulus program," Callahan said, "there will be a lot of claimants. There will also be advocates of greater expenditures for highways, bridges, and other types of public projects."

He suggested, too, that another major issue, such as health care, could overshadow infrastructure problems. "Legislatures," he said, "rarely can handle more than one or two crises in any one session. If health care jumps out of the box early, some of the bloom may be off the economic stimulus package."

Callahan reviewed proposals that surface in each session of Congress, and in state and local government budget deliberations, to distinguish between operating expenditures and capital expenditures. "If we could somehow establish a capital budget at the federal level, we would all be better off," he said. "Financing judicial facilities would become easier."

Lack of a true consensus about what should be in a capital budget complicates the debate, he said. "Indeed when you see the discussion start in January about what we should be doing in this area you will see discussion of what we call an investment budget, not a capital budget. Probably no two people will agree on what should go into that investment budget." Some analysts, he noted, argue that it should include funds for health care and education on the assumption that this will improve human capital.

"So the bad news, in one sense, for all of you here is that we probably are not going to make any dramatic conceptual breakthroughs at the federal level in the 103rd Congress that will make the job of planning and financing judicial facilities any easier. However, Senate Budget Committee Jim Sasser has always had a special place in his heart for the judiciary."

Moreover, Callahan said, an analysis by the committee's staff shows relatively little budget waste in the judiciary account. In annual budget resolutions, he added, the committee has recommended to the Appropriation Committee that the judiciary budget be funded as fully as possible. "We feel that efforts to reduce waste should be focused on such programs as the superconducting supercollider in Texas, the space station, and the strategic defense initiative."

DESIGN THEORY

After a day and a half of discussion of techniques, debate about methods, homage to tradition, and speculation about the impact of technology, it was time to fully dissect a specimen of a real, functioning courthouse. So the conference turned a collective microscopic gaze onto the Robson Center in Vancouver, British Columbia, designed by Arthur Erickson Architects Inc., and completed in the late 1970s.

Arthur Erickson, FAIA

Photographer: Douglas Gordon
© The American Institute of Architects

Reconciling Openness and Security

The examination opened with Erickson candidly discussing the thought processes that led ultimately to design of the center. Allusions by a judicial acquaintance to hangings on the streets of 16th century London and Erickson's own vivid recollection of punishment summarily meted out on Saudi Arabian streets made him aware that the administration of justice is a public process and that it can be a harsh one.

An experience he encountered while conducting research for his assignment also helped shape his vision of the judicial process. While examining a holding cell in one of the older Canadian courthouses he and a court aide were accidentally locked in the cell. Thus he gained chilling personal experience of how the accused feel in captivity. He recalled that he began to sense the sordid aspects of criminal behavior and of how it had to be dealt with. The administration of justice, he concluded, required both openness and security, totally opposite concepts. How to reconcile them was the challenge he faced in designing Robson Square, a huge multi-use complex containing a courthouse and all the judicial trappings, in the center of downtown Vancouver.

If the administration of justice was to be open, then the public should have a clear voice in the nature of the forum in which it would be rendered, Erickson concluded. This set the stage for programming for Robson Square. To give the public an opportunity to express its views, the firm developed a model and put it on display, seeking comments in writing. Comments were quickly forthcoming. The respondents wanted more green space—lawns, trees, and shrubs. Erickson and associates provided plantings in abundance. The public asked for water. The designers used water to link the center with an existing courthouse.

The court complex that grew out of this method of soliciting public attitudes

and subsequent close collaboration with judges and court administrators eventually became the revitalized center of downtown Vancouver. Its public spaces have become popular gathering places. Its seven-story-high great hall has been the scene of both nationally and internationally significant events and of personal occasions like marriage ceremonies. Citizens feel no sense of exclusion. Yet the courtrooms project dignity and solemnity—dignity because of the importance of law in our society; solemnity because of the recognition that this is where society's most intractable problems are dealt with and life and death decisions are made.

As a case study, Robson Center raised some important questions for the assembled architects, judges, and administrators, all of them caught up in what they sense could be this nation's most ambitious era of courthouse building. What lessons might the Robson Center provide as the U.S. judiciary tries to fulfill Chief Justice Rehnquist's vision of justice centers?

How might such centers revive the hearts of aging downtowns, as the Robson Center apparently did the center of Vancouver? How can the dignity and majesty of the courts be preserved within a complex that also includes intensely used public spaces?

These were some of the questions raised in the this final session of the conference as a procession of participants assessed the Robson Center from several perspectives.

Views of Robson Square and the new courts

Photographer: Unknown
© Arthur Erickson/Aitken Wreglesworth Associates,
Vancouver, Canada

Lessons From the Historical Perspective

After Erickson's graphic depiction of Robson Center, amply illustrated with slides, it was time to hear testimony from others—critics, judges, and other users. The first witness was William Seale, Alexandria, Va., architectural historian of courthouses and state capitols whose recent work includes definitive volumes on the construction and renovation of the White House and the impact on the mansion from the families that occupied it. Seale's comments about Robson Square—not a critique, he noted—were contained in a review of the history of federal courthouses, a dismal one for the first half century of the republic. He found Erickson's contemporary work on the Vancouver complex "the most imaginative and challenging since H.H. Richardson's Pittsburgh court complex of the 1880s." This seat of the Allegheny County government, widely hailed by critics of this period, spawned a number of federal buildings, Seale said. And he detected an unprecedented contemporary determination on the part of judges in shaping the new building programs for the federal courts.

What, Seale asked, are the lessons of Robson Center? "Does it fit anywhere and provide promise in our story of federal building? Obviously, with the tremendous interest it has generated, it is considered a possible inspiration." The reviews, when it was completed more than a decade ago, were "generally good, even enthusiastic." Some excerpts: "…[T]he overall design is elegant and expansive, function but with elements of fantasy, offering splendid spaces inside and out."—Architectural Record. "[T]he elements connect to each other as if they had been formed from one concrete pour.

The chiseled and draped monolith is designed to project a formidable image."—Progressive Architecture. "The [great hall] and many planted patios, with opulent purple sofas and rich carpeting, make a public attraction of what is usually among the most forbidding kinds of building on earth."—Time. Drawing from a profusion of sociological commentary on Robson Center, Seale cited an essay quoting Erickson as saying, "I am fortunate that I can stand in Canada, a country without a culture and look at the world."

This, Seale noted, prompted an academic writer to object that Canada indeed had a culture, "the culture of mass consumption. Mass consumption is a critical instrument of the modern state for assuring social and political order. Increasing it provides government with its legitimacy."

"Thus," the historian commented, "the new Robson Square with its courts."

Lessons From the Judicial Perspective

The next witness was William A. Esson, chief justice of the Supreme Court of British Columbia. "There is no question," Esson said, "that Robson Square is an ennobling space. It has liberated downtown Vancouver from stifling mediocrity. Furthermore, from the point of view of occasional users—the public, litigants, jurors, and visitors—the building works magnificently. It has a sense of openness; it is attractive, and it signifies that the courthouse is a public place—a place for the public."

Speaking from the perspective of "those of us who live in the building," he continued: "The large courtrooms are excellent. They are well-lighted, have high ceilings, and provide a good atmosphere. The smaller ones are not quite as satisfactory; their low ceilings require that judges sit too close to the lights. Acoustics are good throughout the building.

"The expansiveness of the building causes internal traffic problems. You can walk a block getting from your chambers to a courtroom. With the number of courtrooms increased from the original 26 to 40, the building now is strained beyond capacity."

Overall, however, Esson's assessment was positive. "It has been 13 years since the building opened and it looks as bright as it ever did—better now that the plantings have taken hold."

Lord William David Prosser, a member of the Scottish Court of Session and Chairman of the Fine Arts Commission of Scotland, had the last word on Robson Square: "If you can create a public space that gets even people who don't have to be there to come, that is very, very good."

Lord Prosser also had the last word on symbolism, discussion of which pervaded many conference sessions. "I think, from where I sit," he said, "we are rather overburdened with symbolism. The wig I am required to wear on my head signifies that I am an 18th century judge dispensing 18th century justice to 18th century people. If one holds to the symbols of yesteryear, one is in grave danger of betraying what one is doing. One should concentrate more on function than on the impression one is giving. If one gets the function right, one achieves the right symbolism."

A Retrospective of Design

The conference closed with a courthouse retrospective show, with Professor Wayne Drummond, dean of the College of Architecture at the University of Florida, providing the commentary. Drummond showed slides of courthouses chosen for an exhibit of exemplary courthouse projects built, or under construction, since 1980. The projects in the exhibit, judged by a jury of architects and court administrators, are documented in Retrospective of Courthouse Design, 1980-1991, published by the National Center for State Courts to coincide with the conference. "At a minimum," according to this booklet, "the jury panel looked for buildings that project a dignified image of justice, provide efficient circulation, possess adequate court zoning, provide for the secure movement of prisoners, and generally meet the design recommendations of The Courthouse: Planning and Design Guidelines for Court Facilities," also published by the National Center for State Courts.

On the meeting's opening day, Drummond had cited personal traumatic experiences, as well as highly publicized crimes, in his hometown of Gainesville, Fla., to illustrate the "fragility of society" and to underscore the need for a sense of urgency in advancing an "architecture of justice. " He adjourned the conference with this parting thought:

"Like the preacher who preaches against sin, we are in danger of working ourselves out of a job if we succeed. Isn't our ultimate goal to eradicate the need for these kinds of facilities? "Citing a school dropout rate that "insures litigation," he argued for increased investments in education "to give young people a greater opportunity to participate in our society. I would hope to appear before you in 50 years and say that some of these courthouses (and prisons) are being adaptively re-used as schools."

APPENDICES

Speaker Biographies

Hon. Arlen Beam, judge, U.S. Court of Appeals, 8th Circuit, was appointed by President Ronald Reagan to term beginning in 1987. He was admitted to practice in Nebraska in 1965 and to argue before the U.S. District Court, District of Nebraska in 1965; U.S. Supreme Court in 1975; U.S. Court of Appeals 8th Circuit in 1976; and U.S. Tax Court in 1979. Judge Beam is a former fudge and chief judge of the U.S. District Court, District of Nebraska. He has been a commissioner of the Conference of Commissioners on Uniform State Laws since 1979. He received a B.S. and J.D. from the University of Nebraska.

Judith H. Brentano, RPR, president, National Court Reporters Association, has 21 years' experience in general freelance reporting and has covered technical patent and trademark cases in the U.S. and abroad. She was chosen to cover the Governor's Growth Strategies Commission public hearings around the entire state for Governor Harris of Georgia. Her primary emphasis is on real-time reporting and closed-captioning of TV news programs for the deaf and hearing-impaired. In 1988, she developed the 11-NewsScribe project for WXIA-TV in Atlanta. She has served in numerous capacities with the Georgia and the national reporting organizations. She holds the Registered Professional Court Reporter designation. Ms. Brentano served as a member of the Georgia Registry of Interpreters for the Deaf, and serves on the Georgia Telephone Relay Center Advisory Board to the Georgia Public Service Commission. She has conducted numerous seminars for court reporters and bench and bar groups around the country covering technology, business management, and related topics. She has also presented at the Harding University School of Business on business ethics. Ms. Brentano graduated from court reporting school in Cleveland in 1972, after attending three years at Cuyahoga Community College in Business Administration.

Hon. Richard S. Brown, judge, Court of Appeals of Wisconsin, District II, was the presiding judge for the court from 1983 to 1990. He was previously a practicing trial attorney, an assistant district attorney in Racine, and an intern for the U.S. Department of Justice. Judge Brown is presently a member of the American Bar Association's Commission on Mental and Physical Disability Law and advisory committees of the National Center for State Courts' Study of Computer-Aided Transcription and Court Interpretation Projects. He is a faculty member of the National Judicial College, where he teaches about the Americans with Disabilities Act, and has served on numerous judicial and legal committees at the local, state, and national levels. He is a member of the board of directors of the Cochlear Implant International, past member of the board of directors of the Wisconsin Speech-Language-Hearing Association, and past vice-chair of PROP Inc. (structured help for juveniles in need). Judge Brown is the recipient of the 1987 Implant of the Year—Cochlear Implant Club International. He received his A.B. from Miami University in Ohio, his J.D. from the University of Wisconsin in Madison, and his L.L.M. from the University of Virginia. Judge Brown has undertaken advanced study at the Institute of Judicial Administration, American Academy of Judicial Education, and Wisconsin Judicial College.

Ronald J. Budzinski, AIA, director of justice architecture, Hansen Lind Meyer, Inc., has been responsible for the design of over 45 projects in 16 states and abroad that range in construction value from $2 million to $135 million. He has participated as a guest speaker in many state and national symposiums addressing architectural and site selection issues associated with facility design. Many of Mr. Budzinski's projects have been featured in AIA design exhibitions and have received citations for excellence. He is currently serving as the project director of the 285,000-square-foot courthouse and the 310,000-square-foot detention center for Arlington County, Va.

William Butler, deputy court administrator, Circuit Court, Prince George's County, Md., where he was instrumental in the planning and construction of the recent major addition to the Prince George's County Courthouse. Prior to this position, Mr. Butler had 30 years of experience as a mechanical engineer and contractor.

Henry N. Cobb, FAIA, is a founding principal and design partner for Pei

Cobb Freed & Partners, responsible for major building projects around the world including Place Ville Marie (Montreal), State University College at Fredonia (New York), John Hancock Tower (Boston), Collins Place (Melbourne, Australia), Portland Museum of Art (Maine), Johnson & Johnson World Headquarters (New Brunswick, N.J.), Pitney-Bowes World Headquarters (Stamford, Conn.), First Interstate Bank Tower at Fountain Place (Dallas), and First Interstate World Center (Los Angeles). His current projects include the Anderson Graduate School of Management (UCLA), International Trade Center (Barcelona, Spain), Friedrichstadt Passagen (Berlin), Bearrix Quarter (the Hague), and the new Federal Courthouse in Boston. Mr. Cobb received an A.B. from Harvard College in 1947, attended the Harvard Graduate School of Design in 1949, and received honorary degrees from Bowdoin College (Doctor of Fine Arts) in 1985 and the Swiss Federal Institute of Technology (Doctor Honoris Causa in Technical Sciences) in 1990.

John J. Cullinane, AIA, principal, John Cullinane Associates—Architects & Preservation Planners, specializes in the development of management and reuse programs for historic properties. Between 1976 and the fall of 1992, Mr. Cullinane served as senior architect for the (President's) Advisory Council on Historic Preservation, providing guidance and advice to federal and state agencies, local communities, and private developers on the treatment of historic and cultural resources. Prior to that appointment, he headed up a nonprofit organization in Louisville, Ky., the Preservation Alliance. Mr. Cullinane is a current member and past chairman of the American Institute of Architects Committee on Historic

Resources. He attended the University of Florida and Cosanti Foundation in Scottsdale, Ariz.

Prof. Robert Wayne Drummond, dean of the College of Architecture, University of Florida, in addition to his academic career, remains active in his profession working with several architecture firms and through private consulting. He was previously dean of the College of Architecture at Texas Tech University and head of the Department of Architecture at Auburn University. He taught at Clemson University and the University of Kansas and served as a senior research associate for Rice University as an educational consultant to the College of Architecture and Planning at King Faisal University in Saudi Arabia. Professor Drummond is a former national chairman of the AIA Architects in Education Committee. He served as the national treasurer for Tau Sigma Delta for the past four years and is president-elect of this academic honor society. He received a B.Arch. at Louisiana State University, a Master's Degree from Rice University, and a Diploma of Architecture from Fountainbleau School of Music and Fine Arts in Fountainbleau, France.

Arthur Charles Erickson, FAIA, is a principal of Arthur Erickson Architects, Inc., Vancouver, B.C. Previously, he was an assistant professor at the University of Oregon and a teacher and associate professor at the University of British Columbia. He received first prize in the national competition for design of the Canadian Pavilion at Expo 70, Osaka; the Triangle Award from the National Society of Interior Design of the U.S.; numerous awards for houses and larger projects; the Pan Pacific Citation of the AIA, Hawaiian Chapter (1963) for

outstanding contributions in the field of design; the 1967 Molson Prize (Canada Council for the Arts); and the Architectural Institute of Japan Award for the Best Pavilion, Expo 70. Mr. Erickson has published numerous articles and lectures, including Time Magazine cover article, February 14, 1972; New Yorker Magazine profile, June 4, 1979; and Time Magazine, October 1, 1979. He has a B.Arch., a D.English, and an L.L.D.

Edward A. Feiner, AIA, chief architect, U.S. General Services Administration, is currently managing a nationwide design and construction program in excess of $10 billion of work in progress. He has developed design goals and objectives for the nationwide GSA program. He critiques and recommends approval for designs of all major federal buildings, museums, courthouses, laboratories, border stations, etc., and is responsible for research, development, and establishment of GSA's design standards for public buildings. Mr. Feiner was previously director of the U.S. Navy Master Planning Program, a project manager with Gruen Associates; a Graham Foundation Teaching and Research Fellow at Catholic University of American; and a teacher of architectural technology at Northern Virginia Community College in Alexandria. He received a B.Arch. from The Cooper Union in 1969, an M.Arch. from Catholic University of America in 1971, and was a Graham Foundation Fellow at Catholic University in 1972.

W. Douglas Fitzgerald, corporate director of security planning, Hansen Lind Meyer, Architecture, Engineering, Planning, is a security engineer who has helped design engineering of 67 American embassies throughout the world, three presidential palaces, 28 NATO embassies, and over 25 Department of Defense and Department of Energy facilities and has completed four major courthouses. He has also served as the instructor for the National Center for State Courts court security technology courses.

Michael H. Frawley, AIA, regional director, criminal justice architecture, Hansen Lind Meyer (Orlando, Fla.), is presently the chairman of the American Institute of Architects Committee on Architecture for Justice, and his extensive project experience includes the management and direction of over 35 justice facility projects across the U.S. and abroad. Mr. Frawley has served as an instructor at the National Institute of Corrections, was a featured speaker at the national conventions for the American Jail Association, American Correctional Association, National Association of Counties, and many state associations and has served as conference chairman for the 1989 national AIA Conference on Courthouse Design. he has played a key role in the planning of this year's First International Conference on Courthouse Design.

Geoff Gallas, executive administrator, First Judicial District of Pennsylvania, works in cooperation with the Supreme Court of Pennsylvania, the state court administrator, and three president and three administrative judges. He is responsible for the Philadelphia Court of Common Pleas, Municipal Court, and Traffic Court. Working with many others, including the Vitetta Group, Kelly/Maiello, Inc., and Daroff Design, Inc., Mr. Gallas will help plan and build a new criminal justice center (CJC) with 64 courtrooms. The CJC project integrates design decisions with criminal justice system improvements

and includes a state-of-the-art criminal justice information system using a $10 million city contribution to a unique public-private partnership. He was previously the vice president of research and technical services for the National Center for State Courts; the Institute for Court Management assistant executive director, senior staff Associate, and dean, Court Executive Development Program; and a private consultant. At NCSC, ICM, and as a private consultant, Mr. Gallas has delivered consulting services including space and pre-architectural planning in 32 states for courts, state court administrative offices, executive and legislative agencies and departments, and for-profit and not-for-profit clients, including doctors, hospitals, universities, Indian tribes, and the League of Women Voters. He received a B.A. from Wesleyan University, a Masters from Harvard University and the University of Southern California, a Doctorate from USC, and is a Fellow of the Institute for Court Management.

Glenn Gauger, AIA, director of justice facilities planning and design, Sverdrup Corporation, is responsible for directing resources, planning, and design of major justice projects. From 1982-90 he was senior vice president and director of criminal justice planning of Hellmuth, Obata & Kassabaum; from 1972-81 he was executive vice president of Gauger-Parrish, Inc. Several of Gauger's justice projects were recognized for exemplary design by the AIA Committee on Architecture for Justice/American Correctional Associates Exhibit Program. Mr. Gauger is a member of the AIA, the AIA Committee on Architecture for Justice, American Judicature Society, and the National Trust for Historic Preservation.

Brendan Gill, architectural critic, New Yorker Magazine, revived "The Skyline," the architectural department of the magazine long written by Lewis Mumford. He is the author of 15 books of fiction and non-fiction, including Many Masks: A Life of Frank Lloyd Wright, and has been associated with The New Yorker since 1936. Mr. Gill's chief avocations have been architecture and historic preservation. He is one of the founders of the Victorian Society of America, the Landmarks Conservancy of New York, the Preservation League of New York State, and the Institute for Contemporary Art. He is chairman of the board of directors of the Andy Warhol Foundation for the Visual Arts and a member of the board of directors of the Film Society of Lincoln Center, the National Building Museum, the MacDowell Colony, the New York Society Library, and the Krish Georgian Society. The Municipal Art Society of New York established a prize in his name, which is awarded annually. Mr. Gill graduated from Yale in 1936.

I. Leo Glasser, judge, U.S. District Court, Eastern District of New York, was previously a professor of law at Brooklyn Law School from 1948 to 1969, judge of the Family Court of the State of New York from 1969 to 1977, dean of the Brooklyn Law School from 1977 to 1981, and has been a member of the Judicial Conference Space and Facilities Committee since 1977. He received a B.S. from City College of the City University of New York in 1943, and an LL.B. magna cum laude from Brooklyn Law School in 1948.

Prof. Charles T. Goodsell, is an urban scholar and visiting professor, College of Urban Affairs, Cleveland State University, 1991-92; professor, Center for Public Administration and Policy,

Virginia Polytechnic Institute and State University from 1978-91 (director of Center from 1986-91); and director and professor, M.P.A. Program, Department of Political Science, Southern Illinois University, Carbondale, Ill., from 1966-78. He received an A.B. from Kalamazoo College in 1954; an M.P.A. (1958), an M.A. (1959), and a Ph.D. (1961) from Harvard University.

Jordan L. Gruzen, FAIA, partner, Gruzen Samton Steinglass, has led design efforts in various areas of architecture for the justice system. He was a pioneer in the 1960s of humane correctional facilities, specialized in the 1970s in police buildings such as the New York City Headquarters, and has concentrated in the last decade on the growing field of courts design. His firm is currently programming and assisting in the design of some of the most important new courts in the federal system, particularly the new Boston Courthouse. His earlier work in renovating the Foley Square New York Courthouse and various new county courthouses has laid the foundation for what is now a national practice in this important field. He is highly qualified to enter this new period of courts evolution. Mr. Gruzen is a graduate of M.I.T. and University of Pennsylvania and is a Fulbright Fellow.

Gary P. Haney, AIA, senior designer/ associate, Skidmore, Owings & Merrill (New York), has been senior designer for all of SOM New York's courthouse projects. These include new designs for federal courthouses in White Plains, N.Y., and Charleston, W.Va.; and the conversion of an existing post office facility into a federal district courthouse in Brooklyn. Mr. Haney has also designed a range of different building types, including high- and low-rise office buildings, educational facilities,

and hotels. He received an undergraduate degree in environmental design from Miami University and a Masters degree in architecture from the Harvard Graduate School of Design.

Don Hardenbergh, National Center for State Courts, formerly a senior staff associate with the NCSC, directed the National Center's Judicial Facilities Project, which was funded by the State Justice Institute. In this capacity he prepared The Courthouse: A Planning and Design Guide for Court Facilities. Mr. Hardenbergh was also instrumental in preparing a court facility evaluation checklist and an automated inventory of recently completed courthouse projects. Prior to this national effort, Mr. Hardenbergh wrote the Virginia Courthouse Facility Guidelines for the Virginia Judicial Council. While with the National Center for State Courts, Mr. Hardenbergh was involved in project work that covered all phases of court management including budgeting and financial management, caseflow management and delay reduction, personnel administration and court staffing, court caseload statistics, and facilities planning and design. He was previously a consultant to the Virginia Department of Mental Health and Mental Retardation; served as legislative staff to the Virginia General Assembly; and was a senior legislative analyst with the Virginia Joint Legislative Audit and Review Commission. He also served in the Division of Program Audit of the Governor's Budget Office, Commonwealth of Pennsylvania. Mr. Hardenbergh holds a Master's of Public Administration degree and a Bachelor of Arts degree from Pennsylvania State University.

Ellen Harland, AIA, architect, accessibility specialist, is currently working with the Office on the

Americans with Disabilities Act, Department of Justice. Ms. Harland is a certified official who has worked continuously in the architectural profession since 1956. After spending 11 years engaged in private practice and teaching in Santa Fe, N.M., in 1988 Ms. Harland accepted a position with the U.S. Architectural & Transportation Barriers Compliance Board. She graduated from MIT in 1956.

Carol Hatcher, deputy trial court administrator, Essex County, New Jersey Superior Court, has extensive court administration and operational experience in architectural program planning and design development for court renovation and building projects. Current project involvement includes the renovation and restoration of a national historic landmark—Cass Gilbert Courthouse, a major conversion of commercial space in a second Cass Gilbert building for commercial use, and construction of a new courthouse facility. Carol conducted some of the original research on courthouse accessibility as it relates to the ADA legislation and has published articles on its implementation. Ms. Hatcher received a B.A. from the University of Charleston and an M.A. from Montclaire State College, completed course work for her Ph.D. at Seton Hall University, and is a graduate fellow of the Institute for Court Management.

Harry G. Hoffman, II, facilities/ operations general manager, Administrative Office of the Courts (Kentucky), was previously a county judge/ executive from 1978 to 1985; and city judge from 1973 to 1978 (Mt. Sterling, Ky.); partner/manager in hardware/furniture/ appliance store; rate analyst for Louisville Gas & Electric Co.; accountant; and bookkeeper. Mr. Hoffman is currently appointed to four governor's task forces—Transportation, Welfare, Reform and Local Government Statute Revision, and Jails—and is a member of the Kentucky Crime Commission. He received a B.S. from the University of Kentucky in 1961.

Mary Lu Holter, senior advisor, IBM Justice Applications, works almost exclusively in the justice arena as a system designer reengineering workflow to use technology advancements. Ms. Holter assisted the State of Maryland in the design and implementation of a wide array of court systems, handling criminal, civil, traffic, juvenile, and jury functions. She also played a key role in designing the Maryland State Police IDENT system (an active criminal tracking system). She has also helped develop correctional, probation, parole, police, jail, and prosecutor systems. Ms. Holter is recognized worldwide as an expert on court automation, probation, and policy departments. She graduated from the University of North Carolina.

Hunter Hurst, director, National Center for Juvenile Justice, a private, nonprofit research organization that conducts legal, basic, applied, and systems research. Under his leadership, the center has grown into a major national resource for credible research, policy development, and publications. The NCJJ's data base of case-level delinquency data from courts throughout the U.S. and the automated juvenile law archive containing juvenile codes from all 50 states are valuable resources in the field of juvenile justice research. Before becoming director of NCJJ, Mr. Hurst was director of survey and planning services for the National Council on Crime and Delinquency. He received a B.S. (psychology) and an M.S.W from Louisiana State University.

Suzanne James, court administrator, Seventh Judicial District (Maryland), previously held positions with the District of Columbia Courts and the Law Enforcement Assistance Administration. She also has experience in training, personnel, and in the design and renovation of public buildings. Ms. James is a member of the Maryland State Criminal Justice Information System advisory board and the Select Committee to Evaluate Court Reporting Techniques. She received an M.A. in Criminal Justice Administration from the State University of New York at Albany.

Hon. Michael S. Kanne, judge, U.S. Courts of Appeals, Seventh Circuit, was appointed by President Ronald Reagan on May 21, 1987. Judge Kanne was first appointed to the federal bench by President Reagan in 1982, and served five years as a U.S. District Judge in Indiana until his elevation to the appeals court. He was an Indiana State trial court judge for nearly 10 years prior to his first federal appointment. Judge Kanne currently chairs a judicial group responsible for setting design standards for all federal court facilities throughout the nation. He has served as a lecturer on constitutional law at the College of St. Francis. He is a member of the board of trustees of St. Joseph's College and the boards of visitors of both Indiana University's School of Law and School of Public and Environmental Affairs. Judge Kanne is a past member of the board of managers of the Indiana State Bar Association and was president of the Indiana University Law School Alumni Association prior to his federal appointment. He served as an officer and was president-elect of the Indiana State Judges Association, and also chaired the Judicial Reform Committee organized by that association. In

addition, he has participated as lecturer, panelist, and moderator in a wide variety of legal programs for news media groups, law related organizations, and judges. Judge Kanne attended St. Joseph's College and received his undergraduate and Doctor of Jurisprudence degrees from Indiana University. He also studied at Boston University.

David Kemnitzer, AIA, principal, Einhorn Yaffee Prescott, possesses extensive historic restoration and building renovation project experience, including numerous courthouse projects. Through his extensive work in historic structures, he is cognizant of the Secretary of the Interior's Standards for Historic Preservation. Mr. Kemnitzer is an active member of the AIA Historic Resources Committee, Society of Architectural Historians, American Conservation Institute, and the board of directors for the Association for Preservation Technology. He has been a featured speaker at the Alfred B. Mullet Festival (Columbia, S.C.), the 1988 Historic Interiors Conference (Philadelphia, Pa.), and the 1989 and 1990 Association for Preservation Technology Conference (Chicago). Representative project experience includes: Harrisburg Courthouse, Harrisburg, Pa. (repair and renovation); Dutchess County Courthouse and Annex, Poughkeepsie, N.Y. (comprehensive design services); Steuben County Courthouses, Bath, N.Y. (rehabilitation of historic County Courthouse and Surrogates Court to comply with OCA standards); Albany County Courthouse, Albany, N.Y. (renovation); USDA Hearing Room/Offices South Building, Washington, D.C. (conversion); Department of Justice, ENRD, Washington, D.C. (study for design of new office center); Sullivan County Annex, Monticello,

N.Y. (expansion and modernization including design of new family court facilities); St. Lawrence County Court Facilities Capital Plan, Canton, N.Y. (A/E and planning services to complete court facilities capital plan); and Onondaga County Court Facilities Capital Plan, Syracuse, N.Y. (assessment of existing court facilities for court of appeals, supreme court, county courts, family courts, and surrogate's court). Mr. Kemnitzer received a B.S. in architecture from the University of Cincinnati in 1965.

Bill Lacy, FAIA, architect and design consultant on the selection of architects, is secretary to the Pritzker Architecture Prize. He has served as consultant to the federal judges in the architectural selection process for the new Boston Federal Courthouse and was chairman of the architectural competition jury that selected the architects for the new Israeli Supreme Court. He is immediate past president of The Cooper Union, former president of The American Academy of Rome, past president of the board of directors for the International Design Conference in Aspen, and former director of architecture and design for the National Endowment for the Arts. He is author of 100 Contemporary Architects (Harry N. Abrams, Inc., 1991).

Mr. Lacy brings to various selection and consulting tasks professional credentials as a licensed architect, as well as management and administration skills in the field based on his experience as dean, foundation officer, and, most recently, a college president. Because of his background, experience, and broad knowledge of the field, Mr. Lacy is ideally suited to the task of selecting architects in an impartial and unbiased manner. His familiarity with the work of hundreds of architects

gives him the basis on which to develop and administer a process for the selection of the best architect suited for the particular site, client, and program. In addition, the office of Bill Lacy Design has access to a vast collection of library and slide resources on architects, which is continuously updated. Mr. Lacy is a lecturer and author of numerous articles on design matters. He holds an honorary Doctorate of Architecture from the University of Miami, Oxford, Ohio, and serves on the boards of the Tiffany Foundation and the American Architectural Foundation. Projects in which he has been involved include professional advisor for the Joslyn Art Museum, Asian Art Museum of San Francisco, Louisville Visual Arts Association, Ohio Wesleyan University (new art center), the Toledo Museum of Art (Ohio), and San Francisco Library; consultant to The Eames House (Pacific Palisades, Calif.), National Endowment for the Arts; and design advisor to the U.S. Olympic Committee.

Dale M. Lanzone, director, arts and historic preservation, General Services Administration, oversees the development and administration of historic preservation policy, standards, and guidelines for the agency's 950 historic or potentially historic properties. Mr. Lanzone was formerly a special assistant to the assistant secretary for Fish, Wildlife and Parks; special assistant to the director of the National Park Services; and deputy chief of the Office of Preservation Policy, Heritage Conservation and Recreation Service. He has been appointed to the President's Committee on the Arts and Humanities; GSA's representative on the board of trustees for the National Building Museum, Federal Council on the Arts and Humanities; board

member of Artists Representing Environmental Art; and chairman of the Reston, Virginia, Design Review Board. Mr. Lanzone studied fine arts at Indiana University and the California College of Arts and Crafts and also studied architecture at the Graduate School of Architecture, University of Hawaii.

Andrea P. Leers, FAIA, founding principal and design partner, Leers, Weinzapfel Associates Architects, Inc., is responsible for major building projects including the Newburyport District Courthouse (Newburyport, Mass.), addition and renovation to the U.S. District Courthouse (Donohue Building, Worcester, Mass.), additions to Schmitt Elementary and Northside Middle Schools (Columbus, Ind.), and the Tobin Bridge Administration Building (Boston, Mass.). Award-winning projects include the Registry of Motor Vehicles (Worcester, Mass.); Hanscom Field Maintenance Building (Bedford, Mass.); George Robert White Gymnasium and Teen Center (Boston, Mass.); Cabot's Stains Corporate Headquarters (Newburyport, Mass.); Photographic Resource Center (with Alex Krieger, Boston, Mass.); and the Maine Vacation House (West Bath, Maine). Ms. Leers has taught architectural design for over 15 years, including appointments at Harvard Graduate School of Design (1975 to 1978 and 1990), and Yale University School of Architecture (1980 to 1989). She received a B.A. from Wellesley College in 1964, and an M.Arch. from the University of Pennsylvania Graduate School of Fine Arts in 1966.

Richard L. Lewis, FAIA, principal, Nacht & Lewis Architects, was elevated to fellowship in the AIA in 1983 for design, and has experience in educational, public administration, and criminal justice projects (all in central California). Mr. Lewis received a B.Arch. from the University of Oregon in 1956.

Carl Lounsbury, architectural historian, Colonial Williamsburg Foundation, was responsible for research and review of the restoration of the City and County Courthouse (Williamsburg, VA) built in 1770. He is currently finishing a monograph on the courthouses of early Virginia (to be published by the University Press of Virginia). His major research interests are public buildings, churches, and meetinghouses of England and America in the seventeenth and eighteenth centuries. Mr. Lounsbury received a B.A. from the University of North Carolina, and a M.A. and Ph.D. from George Washington University.

Margaret H. Marshall, attorney and partner, Choat, Hall & Stewart, concentrates on civil litigation. Ms. Marshall was president of the Boston Bar Association from 1991 to 1992; is a member of the Policy Advisory Committee to the Massachusetts Supreme Judicial Court; a member of the Rules Advisory Committee of the First Circuit Court of Appeals, and the Civil Justice Advisory Group to the U.S. District Court for the District of Massachusetts; a member of the Massachusetts Judicial Nominating Committee; is a fellow of the American Bar Association; and is a member of the American Law Institute. Ms. Marshall graduated from Yale University Law School in 1976.

James E. McMillan, senior staff associate at the NCSC, currently directs the Court Technology Laboratory is project director for the Court Automated Performance Standards project, and is involved with the Judicial Electronic Data Interchange

standard. He previously directed information services for the Arizona Supreme Court Administrative Office of the Courts (automated state supreme court, administrative office of the courts, courts of appeals, superior courts, limited jurisdiction courts, juvenile courts, and probation departments). He write LOCIS (Lower Court Information System) which was installed in more than 65 limited jurisdiction courts throughout Arizona. He has worked with the U.S. Department of Justice, Los Angeles Superior Court, National Judicial College, and University of Southern California Judicial Administration Program. He received his B.A. from New Mexico State University, and an M.P.A. from the University of Southern California.

Ralph L. Mecham, director, Administrative Office of the U.S. Courts, was appointed director on July 15, 1985. He was formerly a research and teaching assistant at the University of Utah in 1951; an executive assistant and administrative assistant for U.S. Senator Wallace F. Bennett of Utah from 1952-65; vice president and dean at the University of Utah; founder of the University of Utah Research Park; special assistant to the Secretary of Commerce for Regional Economic Coordination; federal co-chairman, Four Corners Regional Economic Development Commission; vice president, Federal Government Relations, The Anaconda Company; and Washington Representative for the Atlantic Richfield Company. Mr. Mecham is a member of the Federal Judicial Center Board; Judicial Fellows Commission, Administrative Conference of the U.S. (liaison); Judicial Conference of the U.S. (Executive Committee and secretary); Utah Bar Assn.; D. C. Bar Assn.; and University of Utah National Advisory Committee.

He received a B.S. from the University of Utah in 1951, and Certif. in Public Administration in 1952; and a J.D. from George Washington University in 1957.

Todd S. Phillips, AIA, The American Institute for Architects, serves as staff director of the AIA's Committee on Architecture for Justice and Committee on Architecture for Health. Prior to joining the Institute, he practiced architecture in Washington, D.C. Earlier still, he was engaged in cultural policy analysis and programs development activities, chiefly at the National Endowment for the Humanities. Mr. Phillips received a Master of Architecture from the University of California-Berkeley in 1985, and a Doctorate in History from the University of Wisconsin-Madison in 1976.

Lord William David Prosser, sitting justice of the High Court of Justiciary for Scotland, is also chairman of the Royal Fine Art Commission for Scotland, a body with design review responsibilities for significant buildings in that country. A graduate of Oxford University (M.A.) and Edinburgh (LL.B.), Lord Prosser often worked, while an advocate and before his appointment to the bench, on behalf of clients concerned with development and planning matters.

William H. Rehnquist, Chief Justice of the United States, was sworn in on September 26, 1986; and was previously an Associate Justice of the U.S. Supreme Court; and Assistant Attorney General, Office of Legal Counsel. Chief Justice Rehnquist was engaged in the general practice of the law (emphasis on civil litigation); a law clerk for Justice Robert H. Jackson (U.S. Supreme Court); and has been a contributor of articles on legal subjects to various periodicals. He received a

B.A. and M.A. from Stanford University in 1948; an M.A. from Harvard University in 1950; and an L.L.B. from Stanford University in 1952.

Randall G. Rice, president and founding principal, Omni-Group, Inc., is responsible for architectural programming and planning court projects throughout the United States; including the aurora Municipal Justice Center (CO); Deschutes County Courthouse (OR); South Bay Regional Justice Center (San Diego); East County Regional Justice Center (San Diego); Civic Center Criminal Court Complex (San Jose); Solano County Law and Justice Center (CA); and the Indio Hall of Justice (CA). His current projects include the Sacramento County New Justice Complex (CA); New Juvenile Dependency Court (San Diego); and the New Civil Court/ Office Building (San Diego). Mr. Rice received a M.A. in City Planning from Harvard University Graduate School of Design in 1974; and a B.Arch. from Ohio University in 1969.

Hon. James M. Rosenbaum, judge, U.S. District Court, District of Minnesota, since 1985; was previously a U.S. Attorney, District of Minnesota from 1981 to 1985; partner at Gainsley, Squier & Korsh from 1979 to 1981; private practice with Rosenbaum & Rosenbaum from 1977 to 1979; associate with Katz, Taube, Lange & Frommelt from 1973 to 1977; staff attorney with the Leadership Council (Chicago) from 1970 to 1972; and an attorney for VISTA from 1969 to 1970. He received a B.A. (1966) and a J.D. (1969) from the University of Minnesota.

Hon. Conrad Rushing, judge, Superior Court of California, Santa Clara County, was appointed by Governor Edmund G. Brown, Jr., beginning June

2, 1978, and he was subsequently elected. He is a former presiding judge, and practiced in Los Angeles from 1964-65; and in San Jose in 1965. Judge Rushing is the author of "California Mechanics Liens" 51 California L.Rev. 2, 1963; was president of the Santa Clara County Bar Association in 1974; and vice chairman (1977-78) of the State Bar of California Executive Committee Conference of Delegates. Judge Rushing received a B.A. from San Jose State College in 1960; and a LL.B. from Boalt Hall School of Law in 1963.

William Seale, historian of American buildings, is the author, with Henry-Russell Hitchcock, of the extensive "Notes on the Architecture," a comprehensive architectural history of American courthouses included in Courthouse: A Photographic Document (Horizon Press 1978). He is also professionally involved in the restoration of historic buildings, notably state capitols, and in that field is best known for his expertise on historic interiors, their design restoration, and research. His books include The Tasteful Interlude: Victorian Interiors Through the Camera's Eye (Praeger 1975); with Henry-Russell Hitchcock, Temples of Democracy: The State Capitols of the USA (Harcourt Brace Jovanovich, 1976); Recreating the Historic House Interior (American Association for State and Local History 1979); The President's House: A History (White House Historical Association and Harry N. Abrams, Inc., 1985); The White House: The History of an American Idea (AIA Press, 1992); and Of Houses and Time (Harry N. Abrams, inc., 1992). Mr. Seale received a B.A. from Southwestern University; and M.A. and Ph.D. degrees from Duke University.

Hon. Paul Sheridan, chief judge, Virginia Circuit Court, 17th Judicial Circuit, (Arlington).

Larry L. Sipes, president, National Center for State Courts, is chief executive officer and Board member of a national not-for-profit corporation which is the principal resource for state courts in improving the administration of justice. He was formerly a special master, Marin County (CA) Superior Court, overseeing the administration, investment and income distribution of the Buck Trust (assets in excess of 400 million dollars); director of the Western Regional Office, National Center for State Courts; adjunct professor of law at the University of California, Hastings College; director, Chief Justice's Select Committee on Trial Court Delay (CA); director, California Constitution Revision Commission; and an assistant U.S. Attorney, U.S. Attorney's Office (Los Angeles). Mr. Sipes received an A.B. (Phi Beta Kappa) from the University of Southern California, and a J.D. from New York University School of Law.

Walter H. Sobel, FAIA, principal architect and engineer, Walter H. Sobel, FAIA & Associates, specializes in consulting on the programming, planning, and design of courthouses and other judicial and administrative facilities; and state, county and municipal facilities. Mr. Sobel was responsible for the publication (in 1973) of The American Courthouse: Planning and Design for the Judicial Process. He is currently the chair of the Court Subcommittee of AIA/CAJ working with the ABA Committee of the Judicial Administration Division, he is directly involved in the publication of a supplemental monograph to The American Courthouse. He has been a panelist, participant, speaker, or lecturer at numerous judicial-related seminars including National Judicial College, Institute of Court Management, workshops in several states for presiding judges, court administrators, and/or court clerks including Florida, Virginia, and Pennsylvania; U.S. District Court Clerks; and the 1984 annual meeting of NACA/NATCA. Mr. Sobel is currently liaison from the AIA Committee on Architecture for Justice to the ABA Committee on Courtroom Facilities and to the Appellate Judges' Committee on Court Technology. He holds a B.S. Architecture from Armour Institute of Technology (Illinois Institute of Technology).

Kenneth W. Starr, Solicitor General of the United States, Department of Justice, is a judge U.S. Court of Appeals, D.C.; counselor to the Attorney General, Department of Justice from 1983-89; legal advisor to the Civil Aeronautics Board and Securities and Exchange Commission Transition Team from 1981-83; and was an associate (1977-1981) and partner (1981) of Gibson, Dunn & Crutcher. He received an A.B. from George Washington University in 1968; an M.A. from Brown University in 1969; and a J.D. from Duke Law School in 1973.

P. Gerald Thacker, Administrative Office of the U.S. Courts, has been head of the Judiciary's space and facilities programs since October 1987. He was with the General Services Administration, both at its Atlanta regional office and in its Washington, D.C. office, from 1971 to 1987.

His positions at GSA included serving as head of the Public Buildings Service for the Atlanta region, and as director of planning and policy in GSA's

central office. Immediately before joining the Administrative office, he was loaned to the Office of Personnel Management to implement changes in OPM's administrative support programs, including the establishment of a national space management program. Mr. Thacker holds an M.A. from Georgia State University and an M.P.A. (Masters of Public Administration) from Harvard University. He is a lecturer in government on the adjunct faculty of George Mason University in Virginia and of Trinity College in Washington, D.C.

Colin Thom, director of design, PSA Projects, Edinburgh, Scotland, is with one of the largest multi-discipline design consultancies in the UK, with offices in London, Cardiff, Birmingham and Edinburgh. Before joining the Edinburgh Office as design director in 1990, he had previously designed and project managed a number of large law court projects in London, including three major projects at the Supreme Court, Middlesex Guildhall in Parliament Square, the Inner London Sessions House and Kingston Crown Court. An interest in public sector housing led him to London in 1974 to work in regeneration and redevelopment of projects in inner city housing areas. One of these projects, in Earls Court, gained an RIBA Housing Award in 1977. he spent three years in private practice in West London developing an industrial business park on a site originally occupied by the Iron and Steel Foundry of the British Bathworks, built in the early part of the 20th century. Mr. Thom graduated from the Mackintosh School of Architecture in Glasgow, and for some years following graduation worked in the practice in Glasgow which Charles Rennie Mackintosh founded.

Michael F. Thomas, founder and president, Justice Planning Associates, Inc., previously founded and directed the courts planning practice at Carter Goble Associates, Inc. A former court administrator, Mr. Thomas has brought an operational perspective to the courts planning and design practice. That special perspective, and the methodologies and insights which have been developed, have enable him to receive the only AIA Committee on Architecture for Justice awards ever given for planning projects—for the Utah and Hawaii Judicial System Master Plans. Mr. Thomas has also served as the primary programming and/or court design consultant on numerous courthouse design projects, including five of the largest courthouses designed in the U.S. during the last decade—all in the 700,000 to 1,000,000 square foot range. Mr. Thomas is a major contributor to The Courthouse: A Planning and Design Guide, and most recently published a comprehensive volume entitled Courthouse Security Planning: Goals, Measures, and Evaluation Methodology.

Robert W. Tobin, senior staff attorney and management consultant, National Center for State Courts, is a specialist in court financing and has authored many articles and monographs on this subject. He frequently appears before judicial groups to discuss budgetary and financial management problems. He was formerly a trial attorney with the U.S. Department of Justice; and Professor of Government at the University of Missouri. Mr. Tobin received a B.S. from Georgetown University; an M.A. from the University of Miami; and an L.L.B. and J.S.D. from Columbia University Law School.

Lawrence P. Webster, director of technical services, National Center for State Courts, is responsible for NCSC's technical programs. He previously worked for Utah courts (directed data processing, supervised automation of the district and circuit courts and courts of appeal, and maintained systems in the supreme and juvenile courts). He also implemented case management and office automation systems for the U.S. Attorney's Office (Denver) and managed development and operations for the Colorado District Attorneys Council. Mr. Webster received an M.S. in judicial administration from the University of Denver College of Law, and has done doctoral work in public administration at the University of Colorado at Denver.

Prof. Carroll William Westfall, professor of architectural history, University of Virginia, was previously chairman of the Department of Architectural History, a teacher at Amherst College, and on the faculty of the University of Illinois at Chicago and has served as a visiting juror in various schools of architecture, a tutor in the Prince of Wales' Summer Program in Architecture (Rome, Italy), and as a consultant to various architecture offices and preservation projects. He has lectured and written broadly on Medieval, Renaissance, Napoleonic, and more recent architecture and art. He is an author of several books on architecture (art, history, theory, and criticism of architecture), and is currently writing a history of urban form. Professor Westfall received a B.A. in history of art from the University of California in 1961; an M.A. from the University of Manchester, England, in 1963; and a Ph.D. at Columbia University in 1967.

Dan L. Wiley is founder and president of Dan L. Wiley & Associates, Inc., a recently established firm specializing in court operations and facility planning. He was previously a senior associate and principal with CGA Consulting Services, conducting similar work in Seattle; Pittsburgh, Hilo and Honolulu, Hawaii; Ogden, Utah; Lynchburg and Arlington, Va.; Orlando, Sarasota, and Jacksonville, Fla.; Charleston, W.V.; and Knoxville, Tenn., and many other locations. He is a former trial court administrator in the 15th Judicial Circuit of Florida. Mr. Wiley graduated from Florida Atlantic University in 1975.

F. Michael Wong, FAIA, FRAIA, researcher, consulting architect, and founder of Space Management Consultants, Inc. (SMC), is a pioneer in improving the quality of judicial facilities throughout the U.S. Under his leadership and active involvement, SMC has successfully completed more than 200 justice facility projects in 40 states and foreign countries, which range from rural courthouses through metropolitan justice centers, and on statewide judicial facilities master plans and design guidelines. These include development of the architectural program through design collaboration with the A/E design team, specialized construction observation, and post-occupancy evaluation. He contributes insights on functional, aesthetic, technological, and symbolic aspects of each project. Dr. Wong was the associate director and principal of the Judicial Facilities Study at the University of Michigan from 1968 to 1970, which resulted in the publication of The American Courthouse. He completed a two-year Foley Square Court Facilities Project (New York) and, in 1981, he was a contributor and editor of the Manu-

script for Space Management and Judicial Integration, a project funded by the U.S. Department of Justice. Dr. Wong, as principal consultant, revised the U.S. Courts Design Guide, a guide for federal court facilities that was adopted by the U.S. Judicial Conference in March of this year. These texts are widely used by practitioners of both architectural and legal professions. Dr. Wong has served as visiting faculty for judicial facilities planning and design seminars conducted by the Institute for Court Management, the National Center for State Courts, and the National College of State Judiciary. He recently established a private foundation, "Model Communities for the Elderly," which will provide comprehensive planning and design information to practitioners in this field and develop and construct model communities for the rapidly increasing elderly population in the U.S. over the next quarter century.

Hon. Douglas P. Woodlock, judge, U.S. District Court, District of Massachusetts, was appointed for life by President Ronald Reagan to term beginning July 21, 1986. He was admitted to practice in Massachusetts in 1975 and practiced in Boston from 1976-79 and 1983-86. He was assistant U.S. attorney in Boston 1979-83. He was previously employed as a reporter with the Chicago Sun-Times in Chicago and Springfield, Ill., from 1969-71 and was a correspondent in Washington, D.C. from 1971-73. The Judge was a staff member of the U.S. Securities and Exchange Commission Washington, D.C., from 1973-75. Judge Woodlock received a B.A. from Yale University in 1969 and a J.D. from Georgetown University in 1975.

Hon. William G. Young, judge, U.S. District Court, District of Massachusetts, was appointed by President Ronald Reagan to term beginning in 1985. He was admitted to the Massachusetts Bar in 1967, the U.S. District Court (Massachusetts) in 1968, the U.S. Court of Appeals (First Circuit) in 1969, and the U.S. Supreme Court in 1971. Judge Young was a law clerk to Hon. Raymond Wilkins, Supreme Judicial Court in 1967-68; an associate with Bingham, Dana & Gould from 1968-72, and a partner from 1975-78; special assistant attorney general 1970-72; chief counsel to the governor 1972-74; associate justice, Massachusetts Superior Court 1978-85; and a lecturer in law at Harvard Law School 1979-90. He is presently a lecturer at Boston College, Boston University School of Law, Tulane Law School, and New England School of Law. He was also on a visiting faculty at the Pacific Law Institute (Hawaii) in 1987 and at the Western Institute of Trial Advocacy (Wyo.) in 1991. Judge Young received an A.B. magna cum laude from Harvard University in 1962, and an LL.B. in 1967.

Hon. Rya W. Zobel, judge, U.S. District Court, District of Massachusetts, was appointed for life by the President.

Conference Schedule

Wednesday, Oct. 7

8:00 a.m. - Noon	AIA-CAJ Steering Group Meeting
1:30 - 5:00 p.m.	AIA-CAJ Business Meeting
5:00 - 8:00 p.m.	Conference Registration
8:00 p.m.	Opening Reception, Exhibit Hall

Thursday, Oct. 8

8:00 a.m. - Noon **Registration/View Exhibits**

10:30 a.m. - Noon **Introductions**

Larry Sipes, president, NCSC

Michael H. Frawley, AIA

Ralph Mecham, director, AOUSC

Keynote Speaker

Bill Lacy, FAIA, Bill Lacy Design

Noon - 1:15 p.m. **Lunch, Exhibit Hall**

1:15 - 2:15 p.m. **Designing With Uncertainty I**

Introduction by Larry Sipes, president, NCSC

Hon. Kenneth W. Starr, Solicitor General of the U.S.

2:15 - 3:45 p.m. **Vision of the Courthouse**

Moderator—Prof. Wayne Drummond, dean,

College of Architecture, University of Florida

Henry N. Cobb, FAIA, Pei Cobb Freed & Partners

Prof. Charles T. Goodsell, Virginia Tech

Hon. Michael S. Kanne, U.S. Court of Appeals,

Seventh Circuit

3:45 - 4:00 p.m. **Break**

4:00 - 5:00 p.m **Designing With Uncertainty II**

Mary Lu Holter, senior advisor,

Justice Applications, IBM, Inc.

6:30 - 7:30 p.m. **Reception**

Welcoming remarks by Hon. William H. Rehnquist,

Chief Justice of the United States

7:30 - 9:00 p.m. **Dinner**

Featured speaker—Brendan Gill, The New Yorker

Conference Schedule

Friday, Oct. 9

8:30 - 10:15 a.m.

Track 1: Design

Where Do I Sit?

Moderator—Ronald J. Budzinski, AIA,
  Hansen Lind Meyer

Hon. Michael S. Kanne, U.S. Court of Appeals,
  Seventh Circuit

Allan Greenberg

Richard L. Lewis, FAIA, Nacht & Lewis Architects

S. Paul Warren

Track 2: Technology

Americans with Disabilities Act

Moderator—Hon. I. Leo Glasser, U.S. District Court,
  Eastern District of New York

Hon. Richard S. Brown, Court of Appeals of Wisconsin,
  District II

Judith H. Brentano, National Court Reporters Association

Ellen Harland, AIA, Office on the Americans with Disabilities
  Act, Department of Justice

Carol Hatcher, Deputy Trial Court Administrator,
  Essex County, N.J.

Track 3: Management

Project Team

Moderator—P. Gerald Thacker,
  Administrative Office of the U.S. Courts

Glenn Gauger, AIA, Sverdrup Corp.

Gary Haney, AIA, Skidmore Owings & Merrill

Hon. Paul Sheridan, chief judge,
  Arlington County Circuit Court, Arlington, Va.

10:30 a.m. - 12:15 p.m.

Track 1: Design

Guidelines and Standards

Moderator—Hon. Michael S. Kanne, U.S. Court of Appeals,
  Seventh Circuit

Hon. James Rosenbaum, U.S. District Court,
  District of Minnesota

Don Hardenbergh, National Center for State Courts

Harry Hoffman, Kentucky Administrative Office of the Courts

Hunter Hurst, director, National Center for Juvenile Justice

Hon. Conrad Rushing, Santa Clara Superior Court

Conference Schedule

Track 2: Technology

Court Security

Moderator—Ronald J. Budzinski, AIA, Hansen Lind Meyer

Hon. Arlen Beam, U.S. Court of Appeals, 8th Circuit

W. Douglas Fitzgerald, Hansen Lind Meyer

10:30 a.m. - 12:15 p.m.   **Track 3: Management**

Architect Selection

Moderator—Michael H. Frawley, AIA, Hansen Lind Meyer

Hon. Douglas P. Woodlock, U.S. District Court,
   District of Massachusetts

Edward A. Feiner, chief architect,
   General Services Administration

12:15 p.m.   **Lunch, Exhibit Hall**

1:30 - 4:15 p.m   **Track 1: Design**

Design Trend

Moderator—Hon. Douglas P. Woodlock, U.S. District Court,
   District of Massachusetts

Carl Lounsbury, Colonial Williamsburg Foundation

Andrea Leers, FAIA, Leers, Weinzapfel Associates Architects

Prof. C. William Westfall, University of Virginia

1:30 - 3:15 p.m.   **Track 2: Technology**

Courthouse Technology

Moderator—Hon. Rya W. Zobel, U.S. District Court,
   District of Massachusetts

William Butler, Deputy Court Administrator,
   Prince George's County, Md.

Mary Lu Holter, senior advisor, Justice Applications,
   IBM, Inc.

Suzanne James, court administrator,
   Prince George's County, Md.

Lawrence P. Webster, senior staff associate,
   National Center for State Courts

Track 3: Management

Planning the 100-Year Courthouse

Moderator—Geoff Gallas, executive administrator,
   First Judicial District of Pennsylvania

Jordan L. Gruzen, FAIA, Gruzen Samton Steinglass

Conference Schedule

Walter H. Sobel, FAIA, Walter H. Sobel and Associates

Michael Thomas, Justice Planning Associates

Dan L. Wiley, Dan L. Wiley & Associates

F. Michael Wong, FAIA, FRAIA,
    Space Management Consultants

3:30 - 5:15 p.m.   **Track 1: Design**

Preservation and Adaptive Reuse

Moderator—Todd S. Phillips, AIA,
    The American Institute of Architects

John Cullinane, AIA, John Cullinane Associates Architects

David Kemnitzer, AIA, Einhorn, Yaffee, Prescott,
    Washington, D.C.

Dale Lanzone, Arts and Historic Preservation,
    General Services Administration

Colin Thom, director of design, PSA Projects,
    Edinburgh, Scotland

Track 2: Technology

Courtroom Technology

Moderator—James McMillan, senior staff associate,
National Center for State Courts

Hon. William G. Young, U.S. District Court,
    District of Massachusetts

Judith H. Brentano, RPR,
    National Court Reporters Association

4:30 - 5:15 p.m.   **Track 3: Management**

Financing the Courthouse

Moderator—Robert W. Tobin,
    National Center for State Courts

5:30 - 7:00 p.m.   **Reception**

Saturday, Oct. 10

9:00 - 10:45 a.m.   **General Session**—Design Theory and the Robson Center

Moderator—Hon. Douglas P. Woodlock, U.S. District Court,
    District of Massachusetts

William Seale, architectural historian

William A. Esson, Chief Justice, Supreme Court of
    British Columbia

Conference Schedule

Lord William David Prosser, sitting justice,
   High Court of Justiciary (Scotland)
Speaker—Arthur Erickson, FAIA,
   Arthur Erickson Architects, Inc.

10:45 - 11:00 a.m.   **Break**

11:00 a.m. - Noon   **Courthouse Retrospective Show**
Speaker—Prof. Wayne Drummond, dean,
   College of Architecture, University of Florida

1:30 p.m.   **Tours**

District of Columbia Courthouse, Washington, D.C.—This nine-story courthouse encompases 800,000 s.f. and is divided into three modules: an east and west tower of courtrooms and offices joined together by an atrium, a glass-covered skylight in the center of the abuilding, offers public escalators serving six of the eight levels and permits an impressive view of Judiciary Square from the upper floors. In addition to the escalators, four public elevators serve all eight levels. All public circulation patterns are restricted to central corridors leading from the atrium area to each tower.

Judges and court support personnel circulate through a series of private corridors and elevators located along the circumference of each tower. Detained defendants move from detention to a courtroom through a series of corridors sandwiched between floors and served by special elevators. The courthouse comprises 44 superior court courtrooms and trial judges' chambers, one court of appeals courtroom, nine appellate judges chambers, various clerks' offices, detention facilities, witness and juror rooms, and an eating facility.

Prince George's County Courthouse, Upper Marlboro, Md.—The courthouse is a 370,000 s.f. addition to an existing historic courthouse. The addition includes a circuit court, district court, and related activities and provides local office space for specific state programs. Additional elements of the four-story building include a public cafeteria and a 1,000-car parking garage. The complex is designed to accommodate judicial needs through the year 2005. The building is intended to represent a gateway to the town, the seat of the county government. The new building sits directly south of the existing courthouse and provides a large forecourt and

Conference Schedule

landscaped park for convenient access and easy parking. As a focal point, the central plaza provides for the current and proposed transportation system.

The building incorporates exemplary design features regarding circulation, security, waiting, and conference areas and flexible use of courtrooms. The courtrooms are clustered around several public lobbies that effectively disburse the people throughout the building. The use of six judicial suites and conference rooms allows flexibility in judicial assignments and facilitates the expedient use of courtrooms. The spacious jury deliberation and conference rooms are conveniently located behind the courtrooms. The holding cells are easily accessed by both prisoners and attorneys for conferences and are serviced by a prisoner elevator.

Fairfax County Judicial Center—Designed to house both the general district court and the circuit court, the design fosters complementary but unique identities for the different jurisdictions. An imposing three-story atrium at the bend of the L-shaped structure distinguishes the two wings. Three circulation patterns (for judges and jury, prisoners, and general public) ensure safety and efficiency. The general public's circulation pattern extends along the outside wall of the building to maximize the suburban wooded views and minimize the tension of being in a courthouse. The facility accommodates 28 courtrooms and associated support areas and thematically connects to the adjoining detention center.

The facility's advanced life-safety system includes an electronically monitored and activated sprinkler system and a comprehensive smoke evacuation system. When the fire alarm is activated, it immediately alerts the floors above and below the endangered level. In an emergency, voice recordings are played on all floors of the building to instruct occupants on safety and evacuation requirements.

Note: Tours were organized by Hellmuth Obata & Kassabaum.

Audio Tapes Available

Audio tapes of the following conference sessions are available.

TAPE 1	Keynote Address
TAPE 2	Vision of the Courthouse
TAPE 3	Designing with Uncertainty
TAPE 4	(not available)
TAPE 5 A&B	Where Do I Sit?
TAPE 6 A&B	Americans with Disabilities Act
TAPE 7 A&B	Project Team
TAPE 8	Guidelines & Standards
TAPE 9	Security
TAPE 10	Architect Selection
TAPE 11 A&B	Design Trends
TAPE 12 A&B	Courthouse Technology
TAPE 13 A&B	Planning the 100-Year Courthouse
TAPE 14 A&B	Courtroom Technology
TAPE 15 A&B	Preservation/Adaptive Reuse of Courts
TAPE 16	Financing the Courthouse
TAPE 17	(not available)

1 - 5 Cassettes	$9.00 each
2 Cassette Sets	$18.00 each
6 or more Cassettes	$8.50 each
2 Tape Sets	$17.00 each
Complete Set of 23 Tapes (Program #9208)	$180.00 each

Make checks payable in U.S. funds to M & M Media Productions.
Virginia residents at 4.5 percent sales tax. There is no charge for shipping and handling.
All sales are final.

Send your name, address, phone number, and payment to
M & M Media Productions, Inc., 1109 Cottage Street, SW, Vienna, VA 22180.
Questions? Call (703) 255-3263.